Money
and Me

Money and Me

HOW TO MAKE YOUR FINANCES WORK HARDER FOR YOU AND YOUR FAMILY

JONATHAN CLEMENTS

Harriman House

HARRIMAN HOUSE
www.harriman-house.com

First published in 2026 by Harriman House, an imprint of Pan Macmillan
EU Representative: Macmillan Publishers Ireland Ltd, 1st Floor, The Liffey Trust Centre,
117-126 Sheriff Street Upper, Dublin 1, D01 YC43
Associated companies throughout the world
www.panmacmillan.com

Paperback ISBN: 978-1-80409-375-7
eBook ISBN: 978-1-80409-376-4

British Library Cataloguing in Publication Data
A CIP catalogue record for this book can be obtained from the British Library.

Cover Design by Paul McCarthy, Shutterstock image used. Photo ownership Jonathan
Clements.

02

Printed and bound by CPI Group (UK) Ltd, Croydon, CR0 4YY

For Elaine

Contents

Foreword by Jason Zweig

*M*ONEY AND ME may well be the most personal book on personal finance ever written. It will go down in history as one of the best.

Jonathan Clements was born in 1963 and died in 2025. He spent years as *The Wall Street Journal's* personal-finance columnist; later, he founded the website HumbleDollar. Over a nearly 40-year career, Jonathan wrote roughly 2,000 articles about saving, borrowing, investing, financial planning, homeownership, retirement, and other aspects of personal finance. Financial journalism dates back to the early 1700s; thousands of people have practiced it over the centuries, but Jonathan perfected it.

He always understood that personal finance isn't about money. It's about us: our hopes and dreams and fears, our families and friendships, and, above all, the power and pull of our emotions. It isn't just about heaping up the biggest mound of assets; it's about making our lives more meaningful.

Jonathan wrote much of this book after he was diagnosed in 2024 with a rare and untreatable cancer. He knew he had only months left, but he wrote without an iota of bitterness, anger, or fear.

Instead, Jonathan wrote *Money and Me* with his characteristic grace, wit, clarity, and simplicity, as well as all the wisdom of a worldly lifetime. This book won't only make you feel that you know him; it will make you feel that he knows you. When you read Jonathan's descriptions of his plans and expectations, his pride and embarrassment, his quirks and mistakes, what he learned and what he never got the chance to figure out, you will soon realize he isn't just talking to you; he is talking *about* you.

I also write a financial column for *The Wall Street Journal*, and during Jonathan's illness and after his death I received hundreds of grateful emails about him from readers. The most common message among these readers who had never met Jonathan in person was this: *I felt he was my friend.*

Now he can be yours, too.

Jonathan and I first worked together in 1987; I had the honor of being his friend for nearly 40 years. When I read these pages, I can hear his voice over and over again—and his infectious laughter.

In one of our last phone conversations, as cancer raged through his body, he said to me, "Not everything I'm writing now is so great." He paused, then added with a cackle: "But maybe people will cut the dead guy a break!"

I gasped, but had to laugh with him.

I promise that you, too, will laugh as you read *Money and Me*. You will probably cry, too. Above all, you will learn. Luckily, you will be learning from one of the wisest voices ever to teach about money— and about life itself.

Sadly, people are not immortal. But some books are, and this is one of them.

Jason Zweig,
2026

Introduction

MY CANCER-RIDDLED BODY was telling me I had perhaps a handful of months left. So I, of course, decided to write one last book.

No, I didn't write the entirety of *Money and Me* from scratch during my life's final months. Rather, my wife Elaine suggested I pull together a volume that celebrates the words and effort that I've put into HumbleDollar, the website I launched at year-end 2016. The articles gathered here were written by me from 2016 to 2025, but they reflect a four-decade financial journey, one that started in 1986 when I moved from London to New York and joined *Forbes* magazine.

As I've sought to help readers in the years since, I've also sought to educate myself, delving into topics that intrigued me and which often had implications for my own finances. Like many who are new to the financial world, my initial fascination was investing. From there, I meandered through numerous other topics, including homeownership, Social Security, insurance, borrowing, estate planning, behavioral finance and happiness research.

Along the way, I became less interested in the mechanics of personal finance, and more in how everyday folks interact with money. In many ways, HumbleDollar brought this notion to life. To write for the site, I recruited folks with a keen interest in personal finance but little or no formal training. My message to these amateur writers: You may not be a financial expert, but you are an expert on your own life—and that's a topic you can write about with authority. HumbleDollar became a place where contributors and commenters discussed their own finances with a rare honesty.

What shone through: Personal finance truly is personal. There's more than one path up the financial mountain, and people adopt all manner of strategies and tactics. Mistakes are frequent, but they can typically be overcome, especially if you have good savings habits.

I also note that age really does bring wisdom. While younger adults may take a while to find the right way forward, those in their 50s and beyond usually find their rhythm, diversifying broadly, trading relatively little, and focusing their spending on those things they care about most—and their example can help folks in their 20s and 30s to avoid costly errors.

In the pages ahead, you won't just read many of my favorite columns from the past eight years, some of them slightly edited for this tome. The articles are divided into ten chapters, some with a traditional financial orientation—retirement, investing and saving. But the other chapters reflect my changing focus: family, happiness, behavior, cancer. Along the way, you'll learn more about my journey, financial and otherwise. Fingers crossed, what I've learned will also enrich your life.

1.
Family

M ANY OF US—AND perhaps most—spend our adult years jousting with the scars from our youth. I certainly have my scars, many of them left by the endless bullying during my nine years at English boarding schools. Yet I consider myself lucky. My parents wouldn't be considered wealthy, but I still think of my childhood as privileged: Unlike so many others, I grew up with a bedrock sense of security, and I think that gave me the resilience and optimism to deal with life's setbacks.

In addition to those nine years at boarding school, my upbringing was marked by my parents' divorce. But amid the resulting turmoil, I always had the sense that my two brothers, my sister and I came first. Whatever happened, my parents would make sure we would be okay. I think that's why, as an adult, I never bothered with much of an emergency fund and why I regularly kept 80% to 90% of my portfolio in stocks. In the lexicon of personal finance, my risk tolerance is high.

I've long aspired to pass along this sense of security to my two kids. As you'll learn in the articles that follow, I've given a lot of thought to how I could put Hannah and Henry on the financial fast track. As a journalist, I didn't have a whole lot of extra dollars, but I knew the kids had ample time, and that could more than compensate.

Amassing wealth was never my life's top goal. Through school and into my adult years, I was driven less by money and more by a desire for achievement. Still, money was certainly a motivator. That might puzzle some readers: I grew up in relative affluence, and that often dents a child's financial drive.

But there's a good reason I was partly motivated by money. Values are passed down through the generations in the stories we tell. And our family's story is a doozy, as you'll learn from this chapter's first article.

Great to Gone

On February 1, 1888, George Cope died at age 65. Two days later, he was buried in Anfield Cemetery in Liverpool, England, where his younger brother Thomas had been laid to rest 40 months earlier.

Together, in 1848, the two brothers had launched a successful tobacco company, which would be acquired more than a century later by Gallaher Group, then a major UK multinational tobacco producer. Gallaher itself would subsequently be bought by Japan Tobacco.

At the time of his death, newspapers described George Cope as one of Britain's richest men. His estate was valued at £274,923—equal to some $47 million in 2020 (inflation- and exchange-rate adjusted).

Why my interest in Cope?

He was my great-great-grandfather.

In an alternate universe where nobody spent my great-great-grandfather's money, and instead his estate was invested in stocks and earned seven percentage points a year more than inflation, it would have been worth some $270 billion as of 2020—more than the combined net worth of Jeff Bezos and Bill Gates.

But that isn't exactly what happened. In fact, none of my great-great-grandfather's fortune made it into my hands and, indeed, it never reached my mother and her two brothers. Instead, it took just two generations to run through the money bequeathed by one of Britain's richest men.

I tell this story not to elicit sympathy—in any case, I'm not sure there's much sympathy for tobacco heirs—but to highlight a crucial notion: Success often contains the seeds of its own destruction, and not just when it comes to family fortunes. Consider four examples:

1. Successful companies eventually grow so large that not only do they become bureaucratic and sluggish, but also they attract fierce competitors angling to steal their business. Today, we're in awe of Alphabet's Google, Amazon, Apple, Facebook and Vanguard Group. Give it a decade or two, and we'll likely view them as has-beens.

   All this has been made worse by the pace of technological change. As companies grow ever bigger, it becomes more complicated and costly to upgrade to the latest technology—and that creates an opening for upstart competitors.

   Have you noticed how clunky Facebook has become? Do you wonder why Vanguard unloaded its variable annuity and solo 401(k) businesses? You can bet that thorny technology issues were a key reason. Similarly, when I was at Citi, the bankers had to know how to navigate ten different computer systems, partly the consequence of multiple acquisitions over many years. Is it any wonder that Citi's bankers struggle to deliver excellent customer service?

2. Economic booms are undone by the excesses they create. Robust economic growth allows marginal businesses to survive and prompts banks to loosen their lending standards. But all this can quickly unravel if growth slows or inflationary pressures drive interest rates higher. How many dubious businesses and dicey loans exist today? When the next recession rolls around, we'll find out.

3. Investors are often victims of their own success. For instance, winning money managers attract heaps of assets from performance-chasing investors. Putting that new money to work compels them to buy more stocks, including stocks they're less enthused about.

   Almost inevitably, the results of these managers start to look more and more like the market averages—and often far worse.

Why? Managers often notch handsome gains not because they're skillful, but because their particular investment style is in vogue. But no stock-picking style stays in favor forever.

Success isn't just poison for market-beating money managers. If investors—whether professional or amateur—are making money because of a rising market, they often imagine they know what they're doing, even if their results are no better than the market averages. We saw this during the housing market of the early 2000s, and we've seen it repeatedly in the stock market.

Problem is, this ballooning self-confidence can lead folks to take ever-increasing risk. They might buy a fistful of rental properties with little or nothing down, shift more of their portfolio into stocks, purchase shares with margin debt or concentrate their bets on an ever-narrower slice of the stock market. But what happens when the market turns lower? Even if these investors aren't panicked by tumbling prices, they may be forced to sell by their need for cash or by the leverage they took on.

4. Why do great family fortunes rarely last more than a few generations? Partly, it's because the second and third generation, raised in affluence, don't have the same hunger to make money.

But partly, it's a simple matter of brutal math. For a family fortune to last in perpetuity and generate an income stream that rises with the general standard of living, the heirs face a daunting task. For starters, the heirs need to manage the money so that it earns an after-tax rate of return that's higher than the pace of per-capita GDP growth, which is the rate at which general living standards tend to rise.

But this entire investment gain can't be spent. Instead, to ensure the family fortune lasts in perpetuity, the heirs must take a sum each year equal to the increase in per-capita GDP and leave it in the portfolio to continue growing. That annual amount might equal 4% of the portfolio's value. Problem is, if the heirs do that, it can leave precious little to spend. To make matters worse, the annual amount available to each beneficiary will shrink if the number of heirs grows with each new generation.

How likely are the heirs to make the necessary sacrifices, so the family fortune stays intact? Have I told you about my great-great-grandfather?

Nerd Gone Wild

It's long been an idea that's captured my imagination: Get a child invested in the stock market at a young age and then leave compounding to work its magic. If stocks notch four percentage points a year more than inflation—which many would consider a conservative estimate—$10,000 invested at birth would be worth $230,500 at age 80. That sort of success would, I suspect, give a significant boost to parental popularity.

When my kids were born, I set out to turn this nerdy financial dream into reality. I was on a junior reporter's salary, with a wife in graduate school, so it took a few years to get rolling. But eventually, I settled on a five-part plan to help Hannah, born in 1988, and Henry, born four years later.

What were the five parts? I'd make sure Hannah and Henry graduated college debt-free, give them $5,000 upon graduation, $20,000 for a house down payment, $25,000 for retirement and $5,000 toward a wedding or at age 30, whichever came first. I didn't have this sort of money lying around, so it took many years of regular savings to hit these targets.

For the graduation and wedding money, I didn't set up separate accounts. Instead, those sums sat in my money-market fund. Meanwhile, college costs were partly covered by money I had socked away first in custodial accounts and later 529 college savings plans, once those became available. Still, I probably paid three-quarters of college costs out of current income.

What about the $20,000 in house money? Hannah's and Henry's

11

future down payments went into Vanguard Group target-date retirement funds. The target funds kept things simple, offering a diversified portfolio in a single mutual fund. On top of that, I knew the funds would become less risky over time—an appealing attribute, because I wanted the money easing out of stocks as the day approached when the kids might purchase a home.

I bought both funds in custodial accounts. That wouldn't be a smart move if you thought your children had a shot at receiving college financial aid, because custodial accounts weigh heavily against you in the aid formulas. But I was confident our family wouldn't qualify. Hannah cashed in her target-date fund in 2015, when she bought her house in Philadelphia. I provided additional help by writing a private mortgage for her.

What about the $25,000 in retirement money? That was trickier. To contribute to an individual retirement account, you need earned income. I've heard of parents who have funded Roth IRAs for their children, based on income that the kids earned from babysitting and mowing lawns.

Neither of my children earned much money until they were well into their teenage years, so I went hunting for a tax-deferred account that didn't require earned income. Result: When Hannah was age nine and Henry was five, I opened a Vanguard variable annuity for each of them.

Variable annuities, of course, can have horribly high investment expenses. But Vanguard's offering—which is now overseen by Transamerica—is an exception. The variable annuities were set up as custodial accounts, with me as custodian. Once Hannah and Henry turned 21, I transferred the accounts into their names.

Later, when they started earning money, I opened Roth IRAs for them. A Roth is obviously preferable—expenses should be lower and you get tax-free growth, versus the variable annuity's tax-deferred growth. Still, for younger kids, a low-cost variable annuity strikes me as an intriguing option: They'll enjoy tax deferral on a grand scale—

and the tax penalty will discourage them from cashing in the account before age 59½. One additional feature I like: Their variable annuities allow automatic rebalancing. That means Hannah and Henry's accounts will likely stay on the course that I set many years ago—without further involvement on my part.

Pay it Forward

Mindful. Intentional. Purposeful. These are the buzzwords of our time—and they make me slightly queasy, with their whiff of self-centered, self-satisfied self-indulgence.

Yet it seems those are my goals.

On Monday, a moving van will arrive to take my worldly possessions to a house in Philadelphia that, I hope, will be my last. All this has made me ponder what I want from the years that remain. Three items top my wish list:

1. Do good work

My ambitions today are far more circumscribed than they were in my 20s. A few decades jousting with the world will do that to you. Still, I remain anxious to serve others as best I can—and HumbleDollar is my chosen vehicle.

2. Find some balance

A friend recently called me a workaholic. It's a label I resist, because it's my choice to log long hours at my laptop—and I do so because I love my work. Still, I readily concede my life is somewhat unbalanced, and I want to find a way to work less and spend more time exploring the world, whether it's through books, encounters with others, on bicycle or via airplane.

3. Help my family

As longtime readers know, teaching my kids about money—and helping them financially—has been an enduring passion. In November, the list of family members I hope to help will grow by one, with the arrival of my first grandchild.

This is a key reason for my move to Philadelphia. My new home will be ten blocks from my daughter and son-in-law. I want to help out as best I can with my grandson. (Yes, the sonogram says it's a boy.)

For many, the world is harsh. The government has an important role to play in taking the edge off that harshness. As someone who has benefited from an economic system that creates both winners and losers, I don't begrudge the taxes I pay to support that government safety net.

Still, I don't want my financial security to depend on a large, faceless bureaucracy—I can't imagine many do—which is why I'm heavily focused on the safety net that family can offer. Got a spouse, parents, children and others who you consider close family? You are, I would argue, among each other's greatest assets and liabilities.

How far would you go in helping other family members financially—and how much help would they provide you?

This, I realize, is a topic where many folks have strong opinions. Some believe they shouldn't provide too much financial assistance to their children or other family members, because they fear such help will dent ambition and create an unhealthy dependence. Similarly, others shy away from family loans, because they worry the money borrowed won't get repaid and will leave all involved with bruised feelings.

Much, I suspect, should hinge on a clear-eyed assessment of your fellow family members' money habits. My children, siblings and mother are all remarkably sensible about financial matters, and I wouldn't hesitate to lend money to any of them. Indeed, I lent money to my daughter so she could buy her current home, and my mother has twice made me short-term loans to help with a house purchase.

Not inclined to make family loans, help your children fund Roth

IRAs, subsidize their 401(k) contributions or provide other direct financial support? Even so, I'd encourage you to ponder the concept captured by the title of this article: Pay it forward.

I won't bequeath enough to my children for them to live in the lap of luxury, with no need to ever work again, and—even if I had that sort of wealth—I don't think it would be desirable. But I'm endeavoring to give my kids something I consider even more valuable: a sense of financial security.

While I'm alive, they know I'd bail them out if financial misfortune befell them—and, upon my death, they should inherit enough to provide them with a healthy financial backstop. In other words, as harsh as the world can be, my kids should never suffer the full financial impact of that harshness.

I readily concede there's an unfairness to this: Only those who enjoy some financial success have the opportunity to bequeath a sense of financial security to future generations. But I make no apologies. I've come to realize that financial happiness lies not in a bigger house or a faster car, but in knowing all will be okay, even if we're hit with rough financial times. That's my gift to my children. My hope: With the money they inherit from me, they too will pay it forward to the generation that follows.

Think of the Children

Roughly a quarter of my investment portfolio sits in three Roth retirement accounts. Ever since I first funded a Roth a dozen years ago, I've thought of this as money I'd avoid spending for as long as possible, so I milk maximum gain from the tax-free growth. But lately, it's dawned on me that it's highly unlikely I'll ever dip into these accounts—and that realization has triggered a slew of investment decisions.

My Roth accounts are all at Vanguard Group. Because a Roth's growth is tax-free, that's the place where you want to earn your portfolio's highest returns—and that's why I have my Roth accounts invested 100% in stocks.

But until recently, I managed my Roth accounts as part of my overall investment portfolio. That meant I used my Roth to own part of my portfolio's allocation to, say, small-cap value stocks, small-cap international stocks, emerging markets and so on.

Now that I realize I'll almost certainly never spend my Roth accounts, and instead they'll go to my two children, I've changed my approach. In essence, I'm now managing two portfolios—the Roth accounts that my kids will inherit and the rest of my portfolio, almost all in a traditional IRA, which will fund my own retirement.

To be sure, a Roth isn't quite as good an inheritance as it once was because, in 2019, Congress nixed the ability for many beneficiaries to draw down inherited IRAs over their lifetime. Still, for my kids, my Roth accounts will come free of income taxes, plus they could get ten more years of tax-free growth from the accounts after my death.

Meanwhile, as I've written about before, I'm aiming to simplify my investment portfolio—and, indeed, my overall financial life—as I look ahead to retirement. In my recent portfolio revamping, I didn't change my asset allocation. I still have the same percentage in U.S. stocks, foreign shares and bonds, and I kept my various portfolio tilts, such as overweighting smaller companies, value stocks and emerging markets.

But I moved all of these portfolio tilts to my traditional IRA—and invested each of my three Roth accounts entirely in one fund. It's a fund I believe I'll be happy to hold for the rest of my life, and this part of my portfolio shouldn't require any maintenance whatsoever.

The fund: Vanguard Total World Stock Index Fund.

The fund is, I believe, the ultimate in stock market diversification. With it, you get exposure to every stock around the world of any significance. Right now, the fund has roughly 60% in U.S. stocks, 30% in developed foreign markets and 10% in emerging markets. It represents the global market portfolio for stock investors—a single fund that holds what all other stock investors hold and in the percentages that they collectively hold them.

Does my strategy have drawbacks? I can think of five:

1. I may be wrong and end up needing the money. This doesn't strike me as a huge issue. Until I shuffle off this mortal coil, the money remains mine and, if it looks like I'll need to tap my Roth, I should have plenty of warning, so I can dial down the risk level.

2. In terms of fund expenses, it would be slightly cheaper to own a separate total U.S. stock market index fund and a total international stock index fund. But I'm happy to pay a few more pennies each year per $100 for simplicity.

3. I'll miss out on the potential performance bonus that could come from earmarking, say, 60% for U.S. stocks and 40% for foreign stocks, and thereafter regularly rebalancing back to those target percentages, thus selling high and buying low. But again, for this

money, my goal is simplicity and zero ongoing maintenance, plus the rebalancing bonus isn't guaranteed.

4. My less rational side—the part that thinks it has some sense of where markets are headed—feels Vanguard Total World is too exposed to the U.S. market and to the biggest U.S. stocks, especially tech companies. But the fact is, Vanguard Total World reflects the collective judgment of all stock investors around the world. They've voted with their buys and sells, and this is what they've chosen to own. Who am I to question their judgment?

5. Congress could institute required minimum distributions for Roth IRAs, which means I'd be forced to draw down the account. I hope that doesn't happen, but there isn't a whole lot I can do about it.

Many—and perhaps most—parents strive to leave behind something of value for their kids. I can't give my kids full financial security and, in any case, I'm not sure that's desirable, because we all need something to strive for. But I can give them the sense that, down the road, a financial safety net awaits them.

Delusions of Immortality

We're all constrained by the income we have and the wealth we've either amassed or had handed to us. Result: Those on low incomes struggle to cover daily expenses. The middle class pay for today, while also socking away money for their own future. What about the rich? They often use their wealth not only for themselves, but also to help future generations.

These are, of course, gross generalizations. Some folks on low incomes manage to save surprising sums for their own retirement. The middle class may not bequeath great gobs of money to their children, but they often help with college costs. And, over the years, many spectacularly rich families have shown an alarming ability to devour wealth, leaving precious little for their children and grandchildren.

Still, I am fascinated by the possibility of helping future generations and the small sliver of immortality it offers. "I never knew my great grandparents, but I couldn't have gone to college without their foresight," has a nice ring to it. We may be gone, but it's comforting to think we aren't totally forgotten.

I have helped my two children financially—a topic I've written about frequently. But what about subsequent generations? When I first pondered the issue, I had high hopes: I might not be able to commit significant sums to help later generations, but decades of investment compounding could potentially compensate.

The more I've thought about it, the less promising the prospects seem—and the less surprised I am by the disappearance of great family fortunes. That doesn't mean we shouldn't try to help future generations. But our impact is likely to be limited and short-lived, for two reasons.

Problem No. 1:
The math is against us

Efforts to pass wealth down through the generations face two obstacles: rising living standards and growing families.

As investors, we often focus on outpacing the twin threats of inflation and taxes. If we aren't overcoming those two threats, our money isn't growing. Seems reasonable? In truth, it's a tad more complicated.

Our national standard of living is pegged not to inflation, but to per-capita economic growth. Over the past 50 years, U.S. per-capita economic growth has climbed 1.8 percentage points a year faster than inflation. In other words, if our income simply rose with inflation, our standard of living might stay the same, but we'd feel increasingly poor compared to our ever more affluent neighbors.

This need to keep pace with rising living standards creates big problems for family fortunes. Imagine we bequeathed $1 million, with the goal of generating income for our family in perpetuity. Our heirs invest the entire sum in global stocks, an obviously risky strategy, and we'll assume they incur no investment costs. Stocks go on to earn 6% a year, or four percentage points more than the 2% annual inflation rate. That's a reasonable long-run forecast for stocks, I believe.

In the first year, the $1 million we bequeath earns $20,000 in dividends. Federal and state income taxes would be owed. Let's say that amounts to a combined rate of 15%–18% for federal taxes and 3% for state taxes—leaving our heirs about $16,000 to spend.

Our heirs would need to reinvest the rest of that money to keep the portfolio growing. How much should they reinvest? Suppose the goal is to ensure the portfolio kicks off an income stream that rises not with the 2.0% inflation rate, but with per-capita economic growth.

The portfolio needs to grow by $38,000 to keep up with both 2.0% inflation and 1.8% real economic growth; these total only slightly less than the portfolio's $40,000 capital appreciation.

The good news: If our heirs stick to that 2.0% annual withdrawal rate, both the $1 million and the income it generates will rise every year along with per-capita economic growth, and it'll do so in perpetuity. The bad news: Our heirs will receive pitifully little income.

To make matters worse, there's a good chance we'll leave behind a growing clan. Let's assume we have two children, they each have two children, and those children each have two kids. That means we will have eight great-grandchildren, all vying for their piece of the 1.1%.

You don't need to be a genius to figure out what happens: A whole lot more than 1.1% gets spent, at which point the money we left behind won't last in perpetuity. Instead, it will be depleted, slowly at first and then ever faster, as the demands for income outstrip the portfolio's investment gains.

Problem No. 2:
Money saps financial ambition

Potentially, our goal of helping our family in perpetuity could still come to fruition—if our heirs viewed their inheritance not as a financial mainstay, but as a nice annual supplement to the income they earn from their jobs.

On that score, however, we're running up against human nature. Money doesn't necessarily kill all ambition. But it seems to put a big dent in financial ambition.

I see this with my two children. They won't inherit huge sums and don't expect to. But they have grown up in comfortable upper-middle-class households, and that's had an impact.

How so? They're ambitious—but they don't appear to be especially ambitious when it comes to making money. You can find that raw moneymaking desire among kids from affluent homes, but you're far more likely to see it among those who grew up with too little.

I'm heartened that my children are, for the most part, careful spenders. That should help them avoid major financial headaches. But what about their lack of financial drive? Initially, I viewed it with some concern. But over time, I have come to see it as a luxury that comes with affluence: They worry less about money than I did when I was their age, and that strikes me as a good thing.

Indeed, I have come to believe that, as long as they devote their days to work that benefits those around them, they are leading good lives, even if they aren't collecting big paychecks. But there's an obvious financial impact: To the extent that I leave them money, it'll likely be spent and not passed along to the next generation.

2.
Saving and Spending

Some people are so innately frugal that, even as children, they save money. That wasn't me. Not even close. If any money found its way into my young hands, it didn't stay there for long.

That continued into college. I'd overspend during the academic year, adding to the balance on my credit card. The bank was more than happy to accommodate my spendthrift ways, regularly raising my card's credit limit without me asking. I'd then use my summer earnings to pay off the card balance, leaving me with a little cash for the academic year ahead. That would soon be spent, and I'd be back to carrying a card balance.

My overspending continued during my post-college year working in London. That was when I discovered how much it costs to live in a big city and how little fledgling journalists earn. In August 1986, a year after graduation, I moved to the New York City area, arriving with Molly, my graduate-student fiancée, and £1,000 in credit card debt.

Molly and I called these the "lean years," and they were. I soon had not just a wife, but a child. I needed to grow up financially—and fast. An unexpected bill would cause me panic. Takeout pizza on Friday night was a questionable extravagance. Eating at a restaurant would have me toting up the bill as each dish was ordered. This was not good for digestion.

I often say that good savings habits are the key to financial success. It was a lesson I learned first-hand, and perhaps learned too well. Long after I had ample savings set aside, I clung to the purse strings with an iron grip.

It was only in the last five years of my life that I began to spend freely, regularly eating out and traveling more, even opting for business class on transatlantic flights. Do I regret my earlier penny-pinching ways? Perhaps a little.

But my frugality also meant I could spend the last dozen years of my life doing as I wished. My ballooning portfolio allowed me to think less about my own finances, and focus more on doing the things I love. On top of that, the higher spending during my final years seemed especially sweet. If you've always flown first class, it likely won't seem all that special. What if you've spent your life in economy? Trust me, it's a thrill when you find yourself at the front of the plane.

What Our Dollars Buy

When we spend money, we're looking to get something in return. But what? Forget classic budgeting categories like housing, food, utilities, insurance and entertainment. Instead, suppose we used a completely different classification system—one that reflected the physical, social and emotional benefits we garner.

The list below is, I suspect, far from complete. Moreover, as you'll see, while an expenditure might fall predominantly into one category, it often touches on other categories as well. Still, I find this an interesting exercise.

Why do we spend as we do?

Here are 11 possible motivations:

1. To satisfy basic needs

This is the biggest driver of spending in less affluent nations. Even in the U.S., many folks will claim their spending is driven largely by their needs and those of their family.

But do our needs really determine the bulk of our spending? Count me among the skeptics. If we're talking basic needs—satisfying hunger and thirst, protecting ourselves from heat and cold, getting from one place to another—such spending likely accounts for a relatively modest portion of most U.S. households' monthly expenditures.

2. To feel more secure today

This is the reason we stash dollars in our emergency fund, pay those insurance premiums and plan our estate. It also shows up in other expenditures, such as the safety features of the cars we buy, the purified water we purchase and the home alarm systems we install. How much do each of us value a sense of safety? All we need do is look at where our dollars go.

3. To give us hope

We all want a better future for ourselves and those we love. This drives the education costs we incur and the causes we choose to support. But its greatest manifestation is the money we save each month for long-term goals, notably retirement.

4. To forge stronger social bonds

Much discretionary spending is devoted to building social connections, whether it's taking the family on vacation, going out to dinner with friends, flying across the country to see the grandchildren or picking up the tab on that first date.

5. To brighten our mood

We humans devote a surprising amount of time and money to trying to change how we feel. Some folks go on spending sprees to cheer themselves up. Others drink alcohol to relax after a hard day at the office. We might take a vacation to recharge after months of working long hours. Or play video games and watch TV to break the monotony of everyday life. Or go to amusement parks, visit casinos and day-trade stocks to make life more exciting.

6. To improve our health and beauty

I'm not just thinking about visiting the doctor or hairdresser. Our desire to live a longer, healthier life—and look good along the way—drives spending on personal trainers, make-up, organic food, spinning classes, manicures, Weight Watchers and exercise equipment. Such spending is often accompanied by a large time commitment. Indeed, I figure exercising—bicycling in the morning, taking an afternoon walk and so on—probably devours at least 90 minutes of my day, and sometimes more.

7. To make us wiser

Many folks devote large sums to learning more about themselves and the world around them. These dollars might be lavished on education, books, therapy, museum visits, travel and more.

8. For the pleasure of helping others

When we give to charity or volunteer our time, are we acting solely out of altruism or are we trying to make ourselves feel more worthy? Whatever our motivation, giving is a large budget item for many folks, and for that we're all better off.

Such giving extends to family and friends. Indeed, I expect my financial gifts to my children and grandchildren will easily rank as this year's largest "expenditures." The gifts will make them happier—but not, I suspect, as happy as the giving will make me.

9. To impress others

Arguably, there's an element of signaling to every dollar we spend. With our purchases, we're looking to tell the world who we are and what we value. Even frugality is a form of signaling, though the price tag is certainly smaller than for the conspicuous consumption that many of us disdain.

10. To enjoy a sense of accomplishment

If we have a job, we can have a pleasurable sense of progress and get paid at the same time. That sense of accomplishment can be so enjoyable that people will spend money to get a taste of it even during their non-work time.

Think about the folks who take hiking vacations, run marathons, volunteer, undertake home improvement projects, and spend hours on arts and crafts. Such activities feel like a worthy way to spend time and money—the sort of things we'll gladly tell the neighbors about, rather than revealing that we spent the afternoon binge-watching Netflix. The good news: Among the budget items listed here, seeking a sense of accomplishment is typically one of life's great bargains.

11. To honor earlier generations

Whether we realize it or not, a lot of our spending is influenced by our parents and grandparents. That's undoubtedly true for me. It's the reason I make cottage pie, own antiques, occasionally drink mojitos, order wiener schnitzel whenever it's on the menu, and make a point of regularly visiting England.

To be sure, mojitos—which my father had a fondness for—are not so expensive, while a trip to England certainly is. But either way, such things have a meaning for me that goes far beyond their obvious attributes.

Future Shock

Why do we make spending decisions that we later regret? Yes, we tend to live for today and give scant thought to tomorrow. But it's more complicated than that—which brings me to four insights from psychology.

I find these insights fascinating, in part because they describe how I behave with uncanny accuracy. Many of you, I suspect, will also catch a glimpse of your own behavior.

Moral licensing

If we do something good—exercise, give to charity, work late, purchase an eco-friendly product—we often give ourselves permission to do something that's not so good, such as rewarding ourselves with junk food or a new pair of shoes. In fact, research has found that simply thinking about doing something good, even if we don't follow through, can prompt not-so-good behavior.

This is certainly a mindset I have. If I've been careful about my eating all week, I feel I "deserve" something unhealthy. Two decades ago, when I regularly ran marathons and half-marathons, I'd typically do my long runs on Saturday morning—and spend much of the time pondering the Italian sub and fries I'd devour afterwards.

Willpower budget

As with moral licensing, this is another explanation for why we slip from the straight and narrow. The notion: If we've been disciplined all day—eating carefully, focused on work, going to the gym at lunchtime—we might reach the end of the day with our willpower budget depleted, leading us to have that extra glass of wine or an extra-large slice of pie.

Can we expand our willpower budget? It isn't clear. But if we can take our desired good behavior and turn it into habits—perhaps we make it a point to always exercise on certain days, always have a salad for lunch and always max out our 401(k)—these things may come to require little or no willpower. Our good habits may not expand our willpower budget, but they could free up part of that budget for other areas where we're trying to improve our behavior.

Even so, we'll occasionally find our self-discipline at a low ebb. If you're like me, you have much more discipline early in the workweek—and far less come Friday, when pizza, a movie and a glass of wine prove irresistible.

Signaling

We're constantly projecting an image of ourselves to others with the possessions we buy and the activities we engage in. A BMW sends one signal. A Prius says something quite different. The danger: We end up spending money in ways that send the desired signal, but aren't things we truly care about.

I've become perhaps too aware of signaling. When I'm out and about in the world, talking to others, or even reading emails, I find myself paying careful attention to what self-image people are trying to project. Some folks are more subtle than others, but we're all doing it, consciously or not.

End-of-history illusion

In 2020, I moved to Philadelphia. It was a big change—returning to city life, downsizing, buying a place where I hope to spend the rest of my life—and it seemed like the end of a turbulent time and the start of a new, more settled, more tranquil period.

When I mentioned such thoughts to my daughter, she laughed and rightly so. I am suffering from what's called end-of-history illusion. We look back and recognize all the upheaval in our life and how much we've changed, and yet we assume all the learning and growing are now over—and there will be far less change in the future. We are, of course, kidding ourselves: What we want from life will continue to evolve.

One implication: The consumption decisions we make today—the homes we buy, the furniture we purchase, the art we hang on the walls—may prompt a rueful shake of the head a few years down the road. If it's a modest purchase, this probably doesn't matter, because the flared jeans and combat boots will likely wear out before our tastes change.

But if it's a purchase that'll potentially be with us for years to come and that's difficult to undo, we should probably think hard about our future self and how he or she will view today's decision. We're talking here about things like second homes, backyard swimming pools, boats, timeshares—and, of course, body piercings and tattoos.

Small Pleasures

I want to sing the praises of spending—on the little things in life.

We fiercely resist the suggestion that money doesn't buy happiness. Commentators will often trot out the quote—which has been attributed to all kinds of folks—that, "I've been poor and I've been rich. Rich is better!"

I think that's true. But it isn't proportionally true. If you went from earning $100,000 a year to earning $200,000, or your portfolio grew from $500,000 to $1 million, would you be twice as happy?

Similarly, on a recent evening, I found myself alone, with no desire to cook, so I simply heated up a $5.99 pizza from the supermarket. Yes, I admit it, it was a little sad.

The following day, I went out with three friends to one of my favorite restaurants and we spent more than $100 a head, or some 20 times more. The food was undoubtedly better and there were other perks, including the anticipation of a fun evening, the company and the brief reprieve from dishwashing. Still, I'd be hard pressed to claim that the entire experience was 20 times better than the prior night's supermarket pizza.

What's my point?

There's huge variation in the cost of goods and services, but the resulting boost to happiness varies far less. Buying a new Kindle tablet might cost you $100, while purchasing a new car would set you back $40,000. To be sure, most folks need a car.

Still, if the goal is greater happiness, wouldn't it make sense to spend, say, $10,000 less on the vehicle, which would give you savings equal to the cost of 100 Kindles? That way, you could buy perhaps one new Kindle, plus 99 other treats costing $100 or so.

That would almost certainly be a prescription for greater happiness. *Why?*

Because whatever you do with your money, the happiness you receive from the spending will wane, as the initial thrill quickly turns to ho-hum, thanks to so-called hedonic adaptation. The $40,000 car might generate greater initial excitement than the $100 Kindle, but you'll get to indifference—and perhaps even disdain—soon enough.

One of the upsides of less expensive but more frequent purchases: We might be able to afford, say, a small thrill every week or two, rather than a somewhat larger thrill every three years. Moreover, by favoring smaller purchases, we limit the magnitude of our financial mistake if—as often happens—we misjudge what will make us happy.

Like the idea of small pleasures? Here are seven additional thoughts on that strategy:

1. Ponder your purchases for a few weeks or months before pulling the trigger. You may discover that the best part of each purchase is the anticipation.

2. Go for variety. I'm not saying you shouldn't repeat a small purchase that previously made you happy. But try not to do it too often. Don't always stay at the same country inn. Don't buy a Starbucks specialty coffee every day. Don't always go to the same restaurant. If you make it a habit, it won't seem special. If you do it occasionally, it'll feel like a treat.

3. Buy time. It's our ultimate limited resource. Pay others to do chores you dislike, such as cleaning the house or mowing the lawn, so you have more time for activities you enjoy.

4. Don't finance your spending with debt and, if possible, pay ahead of time. You're more likely to enjoy a purchase if you aren't worrying about how you'll foot the bill. For instance, when you book a hotel room, you might prepay, which will often also get

you a small discount. It's also why I like it when family members give me gift cards to local restaurants. I can then focus on the food, without thinking about the cost.

5. Involve people. We're frequently reminded that experiences tend to deliver greater happiness than possessions. Why do experiences win out? A key reason is that others are typically involved. The experience of going to a museum or a concert is a whole lot more fun if we have company.

6. Give to others. We get a surprising amount of happiness from making gifts and giving to charity. Want to make that gift extra special for the recipient? Make it when it's not expected. Your spouse will be happy to get flowers on Valentine's Day. But if you really want to see her smile, buy her a dozen roses today.

7. Another reason to favor smaller purchases: They typically involve little ongoing maintenance and they often aren't worth repairing. That isn't true for major purchases like cars and homes. Yes, some folks enjoy rotating the tires and fixing the leaky faucet. But most of us don't, which is why cars and homes are frequent sources of unhappiness.

The Tipping Point

Starting to save is a discouraging business. Even if you invest in stocks—and even if stocks post gains—progress initially can seem agonizingly slow.

Consider a simple example. Let's say you earn $100,000 a year and you save 12% of your income, equal to $12,000 each year. That money is invested at the start of the year and earns 6% annually, which is my expectation for long-run stock returns.

After three years, you've socked away $36,000 and collected three years of investment gains, and yet your account balance is $40,500. That doesn't exactly fuel your motivation. You've invested for three years and you have just 40% of what you earn in one year from work.

Still, you persist, and in year 12 something interesting happens. By that juncture, you've socked away $144,000 and your year-end balance is a little below $215,000, which means you've now garnered almost $71,000 in investment gains. That's not bad. Even more impressive: In year 12, for the first time, your investment gains—at $12,146—are marginally larger than the $12,000 you socked away.

You have reached the tipping point.

I first heard this moment described by investment advisor Charles Farrell, author of *Your Money Ratios*, and I've been fascinated by it ever since. Your portfolio is now hitting on both cylinders, thanks to significant contributions not only from your own regular savings, but also from investment gains. Thereafter, your nest egg's growth is explosive: You go from less than $215,000 at the end of year 12 to $500,000 in year 21, $1 million in year 30 and almost $2 million in year 40.

To be sure, this happy story hinges on its assumptions. What if, instead of clocking 6% a year, the stock market nosedives? As long as you keep up your regular investment program—and as long as stocks eventually recover—this could boost your portfolio's ultimate value, as you scoop up shares at bargain prices.

We also need to factor in inflation. My expected 6% long-run annual return is built, in part, on an assumed 2% inflation rate, so after-inflation stock returns are 4%. But if we have 2% inflation, that would likely boost your $100,000 salary by a similar amount each year, while also reducing the spending power of the nest egg you amass.

Let's imagine your salary increases 2% annually—and so, too, does the nominal amount you save. After 40 years, you would have accumulated almost $2.6 million. But all those years of 2% inflation would slash the spending power of a dollar by 55%, so your portfolio's value—in today's dollars—would be worth somewhat under $1.2 million.

Getting an early start, and thereby enjoying a full 40 years of compounding, was crucial to hitting that $1.2 million. What if you had procrastinated for five years, so you only saved and invested for 35 years? Instead of $1.2 million, you would have ended up with a tad over $900,000, or 22% less.

As it happens, that $1.2 million is equal to 12 times your annual salary, which is often suggested as a goal for retirement savers. If you have 12 times your income saved by the time you retire, your portfolio should be able to generate retirement income equal to roughly half your annual salary, based on a 4% withdrawal rate. Add in Social Security, get your mortgage and other debts paid off by the time you quit the workforce, and you should be set for a comfortable retirement.

Nice work, right? And all it takes is a little perseverance—through those discouraging first dozen years.

Don't Overdo It

Thrifty. Frugal. Cheap. Pick the adjective you favor, and you could apply it to me.

I've spent almost my entire adult life being financially careful. I haven't carried a credit card balance or overdrawn my checking account since my early 20s. I was an early convert to low-cost index funds. When I worked at *The Wall Street Journal* and at Citigroup, I brought my breakfast and a thermos of coffee to the office every day, and occasionally lunch as well. I run a lean refrigerator, rarely throwing away food because I only stock what I'm confident I'll eat.

But even I have my limits. I'm all for saving money, but some of the articles and comments from supposed savings gurus leave me shaking my head.

Want to lead the frugal life? Here are five thoughts:

1. Cars trump coffee

The criticism directed at millennials, with their supposed obsession with Frappuccinos and avocado toast, strikes me as silly. Partly, it smacks of misguided generational jousting. We shouldn't be surprised that the current generation spends more than the generations that came before. That's what happens in a society with a rising standard of living.

More important, a few cups of coffee pale in significance next to the cost of housing and cars, which together account for half of U.S. household spending. If folks are struggling to save, it almost certainly isn't because of their coffee habit. Instead, they're likely boxed in by high housing costs and steep monthly debt payments, including for cars and college loans.

2. Everybody has passions

To be sure, if somebody downs a $6 specialty coffee every day, the long-term cost could be significant. (Because no article on the perils of high-cost coffee would be complete without such a calculation, the answer is $212,000 over 40 years. The question: How much would you have after four decades if you invested $6 a day and earned 4% a year?)

But what if you really love overpriced coffee? Why shouldn't you buy it? If mocha lattes are what make your heart sing, I see no reason not to buy them, as long as you're saving enough for your various goals. This goes to my disdain for budgeting: If we're diligently funding retirement and other investment accounts every month, it doesn't much matter what we do with the rest of our money—and there's no need to track where every penny goes.

3. Three basis points won't kill us

Over the years, I've received multiple emails from readers, asking whether they should swap from index mutual funds into lower-cost exchange-traded index funds (ETFs). This is a particular issue at Vanguard Group, where there's a corresponding ETF for almost every index mutual fund and making the switch to the ETF might save you perhaps 0.01 to 0.05 percentage points a year. In Wall Street lingo, those fractions of a percent are called basis points.

As I've argued elsewhere, shifting from index mutual funds to ETFs isn't the slam dunk that many folks imagine. While ETFs typically have lower annual expenses, you'll get nicked for the bid-ask spread when you buy and sell. Still, if you plan to stick with an ETF for more than a few years, it's probably worth making the swap.

But don't get too excited about the savings. Suppose that, by swapping to the ETF, you can lower your annual expenses by 0.03 percentage points. We're talking $30 a year on a $100,000 investment.

I wouldn't turn up my nose at an extra $30. But I'm also not going to argue this is a must-do investment move.

4. We save now so we can spend later

Once, at a financial conference, a fellow attendee sidled up to me and whispered, "You see that guy over there filling up a shopping bag with bottles of orange juice from the drinks buffet? He's worth $50 million."

I'm not greatly bothered by such cheapskate behavior. But it does raise the question: Will the guy ever get much pleasure from his $50 million, beyond admiring his net worth's impressive size? We shouldn't get so good at saving money that we can't eventually bring ourselves to spend the fruits of our frugality.

What if we're reluctant to spend on ourselves? I think there's great virtue in spending on others, for two reasons. First, giving to others—whether it's to family, friends or a favorite charity—often sparks greater happiness than spending on ourselves, so it can help us to get joy from money we'd otherwise be loath to spend. Second, by giving away some of our money, we may see that parting with a sliver of our wealth doesn't necessarily trigger financial Armageddon, and that may make us a tad more relaxed about future spending.

5. Excessive frugality costs time

As I've noted before, time is the ultimate limited resource. If we spend hours hunting for the lowest price, we waste precious time. If we track every penny we spend, that's time that could be devoted to something more enjoyable. If we're so miserly that we spend our days worrying about how much we spend, we're taking our good habits—which have the potential to free us from financial concerns—and turning them into the same mental burden that afflicts those who have no savings.

The bottom line: There's a point of diminishing returns in our efforts to save money and accumulate more and, if we overdo it, there's a grave risk we'll miss the big picture.

3.
Markets

I N 1986, WHEN I arrived in New York from London, it wasn't easy for a cash-strapped 23-year-old to get started as an investor. Back then, Fidelity Investments and T. Rowe Price demanded $2,500 to open a mutual-fund account, far more than I could afford. Meanwhile, Vanguard Group required $3,000, and typically still does.

What to do? I got my start by purchasing six individual stocks through the National Association of Investors Corp., which helped investors enroll in the dividend reinvestment plans of a limited number of publicly traded companies. I picked six stocks: insurers Aetna and Aflac, Gulf + Western, grocery store owner Hannaford Bros., McDonald's and truck rental company Ryder.

Subsequently, I tried my luck with a few low-minimum mutual funds, including Twentieth Century (now American Century) Vista. The fund, which no longer exists, made a roller-coaster ride seem like a gentle stroll through the countryside. Indeed, it was the only time I've ever owned a fund that ranked as the top performer for the quarter. In 1992, I sold all these investments, so I could make my first house down payment. Since then, when investing outside employer plans, I've used Vanguard Group funds almost exclusively.

Vanguard, of course, is the leading purveyor of index funds. I first visited Vanguard's Malvern, Pa., headquarters in 1987. That was when I met John Bogle, the firm's garrulous, feisty, larger-than-life founder. I talked to Jack often over the three decades that followed, and he had an enormous influence on my thinking.

Later, when I joined *The Wall Street Journal*, I became known as an early and vocal advocate of indexing. I got many things wrong during my career, but this was one I got right.

I also became known for regularly extolling the virtues of stock-market investing, encouraging readers to allocate a hefty portion of their portfolio to stocks. Amid the occasional gut-wrenching market declines, this wasn't always the most comfortable position to take. But as with many investors, tilting toward stocks has paid off handsomely for me over the decades. Indeed, for everyday investors, I think the road to wealth is remarkably simple, even if it isn't easy: You need to save diligently, invest heavily in stocks, favor low-cost broadly diversified index funds—and try mightily not to panic when markets plunge.

Sharing Lessons

The stock market has been one of my life's enduring interests. No, it's not because I try to pick market-beating investments. I gave up on that nonsense more than three decades ago.

Rather, I'm fascinated by the way we humans engage with this maddening market that promises both riches and peril, and which seems both ruthlessly efficient and utterly nuts. What have I learned from a lifetime of following the stock market? The sad truth is, I find there's precious little that I can say with any confidence.

Indeed, I remain convinced that the best strategy is to sit patiently with a globally diversified portfolio of index funds—an approach that requires no crystal ball and very little trading. That said, on top of this know-nothing approach, I've layered four key ideas about the stock market.

1. Failing to forecast

When I started investing in 1987, grumpy old men would regularly warn that the market was overvalued and that stock investors would soon receive the punishment they so richly deserved. These market "wisemen" would point out that shares were richly valued based on yardsticks like price-to-book value, dividend yield and price-to-earnings multiples.

And yet, as the years rolled by, stocks kept getting more and more expensive, and those who listened to the grumpy old men were the ones who got punished. It eventually dawned on me that investors couldn't divine the market's future by studying valuation measures, and today I pay them scant attention.

2. Holding steady

Every day, the market tells us what our stocks and funds can be sold for. But for the sake of our own sanity, we need a sense of our holdings' value that's separate from the market's latest declaration.

No, we won't be able to figure out what our investments are truly worth. Nobody can. But what we can do is constantly remind ourselves that the fundamental value of our stocks and funds fluctuates far less than their market price.

To be sure, if we needed to sell, we'd have to accept the current price. But absent that, we should focus on what we own—companies with valuable assets that generate healthy profits and often pay reliable dividends—and we should hold that notion close, especially when pundits, panicked investors and plunging prices try to bully us into believing otherwise.

3. Freaking out

When valuing a stock, analysts often start by estimating the profits that a company will generate in the years ahead, or the cash it'll return to shareholders through dividends and stock buybacks. These analysts will then apply a discount rate to the figures for later years because $1 of profits or dividends five or ten years from now isn't as valuable as $1 today. They'll then add up this stream of discounted future earnings or future cash payments to shareholders, and that gives them a company's intrinsic value.

So, what happens to a company's intrinsic value if it gets hit with a big economic slowdown or a serious business problem that wipes out all profits for, say, the next three years, thus nixing the company's ability to pay dividends and buy back shares? Remember, we're talking here about a financial debacle—no corporate profits for three years—

and yet, depending on the assumptions used, the company's intrinsic value might drop less than 10%.

Meanwhile, in a typical bear market, share prices nosedive an average 35%. In other words, when the news turns bleak and investors freak out, share prices tend to fall far more than the decline in intrinsic value would justify. In fact, judging by the size of the typical bear market decline, it seems investors are effectively assuming that the bad news might last for perhaps a dozen years.

Can't imagine the world's companies failing to generate any earnings for a dozen years? When the broad market plunges, maybe what we're seeing is an overreaction—and what we're getting is a great buying opportunity.

4. Making hay

Where does that leave us? It's hard to figure out whether stocks are objectively cheap or not, but it seems that share prices tend to overshoot both on the way up and on the way down.

I'm not inclined to lighten up on stocks when the market appears overheated, because there's no limit to how high share prices might climb. But it's a different story during declines: Shares can't lose more than 100% of their value—and, unless the world suffers economic Armageddon, they won't.

That's why I invest more in the broad market whenever there's a steep drop. No, I don't try to figure out whether stocks are objectively cheap, because I've learned market yardsticks can't tell us where the market is headed next.

Instead, I simply take my cues from the magnitude of the market's decline, and the bigger it is, the more enthusiastic I am about buying. That might sound naïve. But after decades of investing, buying aggressively during a bear market—coupled with leaning heavily toward stocks and favoring index funds—are the only ways I know to get an edge.

Not Scared of Bears

I have no idea how stocks will perform this year or next. But I have full confidence that a globally diversified stock portfolio will fare just fine over the decades ahead.

How do I justify my optimism about the long term? Here are five ways.

1. Heads I win, tails we all lose

I view the stock market as an asymmetric bet. If all goes well, stocks win. If things go terribly, all investments could potentially lose— bonds, cash investments, alternatives, you name it. If we get economic apocalypse, nobody's going to want to exchange their last remaining food and water for your American Eagle gold coins, and they certainly won't want your Bitcoin.

To be sure, the future isn't limited to two alternatives, either continued economic growth or economic apocalypse. Conceivably, the economy could stagnate, generating no long-term growth. In such a scenario, holders of bonds and cash investments might still get paid, even as stocks plunge in value. Still, while it's entirely possible that we'll have a brief period of no growth—after all, U.S. real GDP shrank in 2009 and 2020—I think it's highly unlikely this would continue long term. How can I be so sure? That brings me to my next point.

2. Humans strive relentlessly to improve their lot in life

When Hurricane Irma hit the Florida Keys in 2017, 25% of homes were destroyed and another 65% suffered major damage, according to the initial assessment by the Federal Emergency Management Agency. Did residents give up in despair? Far from it. Three years later, when I drove down to Key West with my sister, the Keys were back to business as usual.

But perhaps my favorite example is 2020's pandemic. Not only was it astonishing how fast a vaccine was developed, but also businesses large and small adapted with remarkable speed to a world where folks were leery of close contact with one another. Welcome to Zoom calls, online Peloton classes, outdoor dining and contactless payment systems.

3. If the economy keeps growing, stocks should keep rising

Vanguard Group founder Jack Bogle would occasionally offer his forecast for U.S. stock market returns over the next ten years using three inputs: starting dividend yield, expected growth in earnings per share, and changes in the market's price-earnings (P/E) ratio.

Let's say we add a dividend yield of 1.5% to the 6.5% annualized growth in earnings per share for the past ten years. Result? We might be looking at stock market returns of 8% a year. But what if investor sentiment turns sour, driving down the market's P/E ratio?

Let's say the S&P 500's P/E falls from 28 to 20. If that happens over ten years, it would knock 3.3 percentage points a year off the market's total return, leaving investors with some 5% a year. What if this "multiple contraction" takes place over 20 years? The annual hit would be 1.7 percentage points.

The lesson: Investor sentiment isn't that important to long-term investors, and the longer your time horizon, the less important it becomes. Instead, what matters is growth in earnings per share. As long as the economy keeps humming along and investors hang tough, they should fare just fine.

4. If the economy malfunctions, the government will pull out all the stops

Have you heard that it took 25 years for the Dow Jones Industrial Average to return to the high notched in 1929, just prior to the Great Depression? If you calculate after-inflation returns and include dividends, it turns out that investors who bought at the 1929 peak would have broken even (at least temporarily) by late 1936.

More important, the economic hit could have been shortened and softened if politicians and policymakers hadn't initially pursued tight fiscal and monetary policies. Those policies made the Great Depression so much worse. Today, by contrast, politicians and policymakers may not get it exactly right, but they have a far better idea of how to handle such situations.

In his book *Deep Risk*, Bill Bernstein points to four such risks—deflation, inflation, confiscation and devastation. These are Bernstein's four horsemen of the economic apocalypse, all of which could do major, permanent damage to your portfolio. Confiscation and devastation—think an overthrow of our democracy or war on U.S. soil—could destroy the value of all investments, whether stocks, bonds or cash. In such scenarios, not much would help beyond an ample supply of food, fuel and ammo. A well-stocked wine cellar might also come in handy.

But what about the other two risks, deflation and inflation? The folks in Washington are keenly aware of both. In late 2008 and early 2020, they moved quickly to head off the risk of deflation. In 2022, they again moved decisively, this time to throttle escalating inflation. All three episodes were a messy business. But without Washington's intervention, they would have been a whole lot worse.

5. It's a big world—fortunately

In February 2024, Japanese stocks notched an all-time high for the first time in 34 years. The country's painfully protracted bear market isn't a reason to be fearful of the Japanese market. Rather, it's a reason to avoid investing heavily in any one country's stock market.

That's why my core holding is Vanguard Total World Stock Index Fund, which replicates the global stock market's weightings and has some 40% in foreign stocks. To many U.S. investors, that seems like far too much abroad. To me—faced with the slim possibility that the U.S. could suffer its own protracted bear market—it seems like it might be too little. But I'm not inclined to stray from the global stock market's weightings. I may be an optimist—but I'm not optimistic that I can outguess the financial markets.

My Investment Sin

I'll concede it's hard to justify—but I don't believe it's 100% unjustifiable. At issue: my strategy of overweighting stocks during big market declines. I did so in 2007–09, early 2020 and 2022.

"Market timer," cry the critics. That, in financial circles, ranks as pretty much the nastiest insult you can hurl, even worse than calling someone an "annuity salesman."

How can I justify this sort of active asset allocation? Let me offer three contentions.

1. This isn't market timing

I'm not making a big all-or-nothing bet based on a market forecast, but rather responding to what the market has already done. Of course, I hope—and indeed fully expect—that the broad stock market will eventually recover its losses and go on to notch new all-time highs. But I have no idea when that'll happen. That's why I haven't made some big onetime shift from bonds to stocks, which is what a market-timer would do. Instead, I just keep buying more as share prices fall, and that's how I end up overweighted in stocks.

I'd argue this is similar to rebalancing, but a tad more aggressive. When we rebalance, we also react to what the financial markets have done, moving money into parts of our portfolio that have become underweighted relative to our targets. I'm taking this a step further, not just getting stocks back to my portfolio's target stock percentage, but opting for an overweighted position to take advantage of the steep decline.

2. Markets overshoot

In academic circles, this is a point of some debate. If financial markets are efficient, stock and bond prices should always reflect underlying value.

I believe financial markets are indeed reasonably efficient. It's why most active money managers fail to beat their benchmark index, and it's why market forecasters show no more prescience than folks guessing heads or tails on a coin flip.

Still, every so often, large numbers of investors seem to fall victim to collective hysteria and share prices become unmoored from their intrinsic value. This appears to happen during major market declines, when fear runs rampant, and that's why I'm willing to overweight stocks.

3. Market returns revert to the mean

In academic circles, this is also a point of some debate. If stock and bond prices follow a random walk, what happens next year should be unrelated to what's happening this year. In other words, if stocks fall 25% this year, that makes no difference to the odds of whether they'll fall 25% next year, and the year after that, and the year after that.

I think this is nonsense. Yes, what happens to stocks on Monday tells you nothing about what will happen to share prices on Tuesday. But if share prices fall for years on end while corporate earnings keep growing, eventually stocks will become an unbelievably compelling value proposition. What if, instead of growing, corporate earnings shrink year after year? In that case, something disastrous is happening in the world—and, frankly, it won't matter what you own.

To be clear, I'm not betting on reversion to the mean by any individual stock, or market sector, or even country. Instead, I'm betting on reversion to the mean by the global stock market. Indeed, my portfolio's single biggest holding is Vanguard Total World Stock Index Fund. What if I was less diversified? I suspect I'd also be less inclined to buy when markets plunge.

Enough Already

"When you've won the game, stop playing with the money you really need." That's something my longtime friend and fellow author William Bernstein is fond of saying. Think about it. If you've already won the game, why would you keep playing?

Risk unrewarded

As I see it, if you own a globally diversified portfolio of index funds, there are only four legitimate reasons to ease up on stocks.

First, you might sell as part of a regular rebalancing program. Second, you might unload stocks as you approach retirement—and continue to do so once retired—as you look to draw spending money from your portfolio. Third, you might sell if you no longer need to take so much risk, because you're financially well ahead of where you need to be.

Finally, you should probably lighten up on stocks if you can't afford to take so much risk because the consequences of a big market decline would be devastating.

But how can you tell if you're taking too much risk?

In a 2015 article for *The Wall Street Journal*, Bill offered a series of benchmarks: You should aim to have at least 25 years of required portfolio withdrawals socked away if you retire at age 60, 20 years if you retire at 65 and 17 years if you retire at 70. Need $40,000 from your portfolio and plan to call it quits at age 60? Bill's rule suggests you need a $1 million portfolio.

What if your nest egg is smaller than Bill's benchmarks? He argues you should favor a more conservative portfolio, perhaps with 60% in bonds. That way, you run less risk that your need for income—coupled with a vicious stock market decline—will eviscerate your portfolio and leave you eating cat food.

Calling it quits

Those who are at, or comfortably above, Bill's benchmarks have more financial leeway and can afford to keep more in stocks. But should you? You've won the game. Should you continue to play aggressively, with a view to enriching your heirs or your favorite charities? Or should you dial down the risk, so you can live out your days knowing that only financial Armageddon could derail your comfortable retirement?

That brings us to the big fear: We get modest long-run stock returns—and we arrive there by suffering atrocious short-run results. That's not a problem for younger workers, who could take advantage of a market decline by buying shares at bargain prices. But it's a grave danger for those near or in retirement: Selling stocks at fire-sale prices, either out of panic or because we need spending money, could cause massive financial damage.

How can we minimize that risk?

Let's assume stocks notch a modest 5% a year and bonds deliver 2.5%. Let's also assume we're aiming to fund a 30-year retirement. We want a portfolio that permits us to withdraw 4% in the first year, equal to $4,000 for every $100,000 saved, and thereafter allows us to step up our annual withdrawals with inflation.

To make it through 30 years without running out of money, our investments need to earn an average 3.4% a year if inflation is 2%. Based on the low annual returns assumed above, investors could hit that 3.4% with a mix of 36% stocks and 64% bonds. The good news: That sort of portfolio should hold up well even if we get hit with brutal financial markets.

The above calculation is, I admit, a tad unrealistic, because it assumes we earn the same return year after year. Depending on whether we get good or bad results early in retirement, we might need a lower or higher average return to make it through 30 years. Still, the calculation tells us that retirees could potentially take very little risk.

And yet I'm not about to cut my stock holdings to 36%. Not even close. Partly, it's because I would like to earn more than 3.4%, so there's more money left over for my children. Partly, it's because my retirement might last longer than 30 years—or so I thought before my cancer diagnosis—and taking a little additional risk should deliver a higher portfolio return and give me a financial cushion.

But truth be told, I'm also not yet ready to quit the game—which suggests that perhaps I'm not being entirely rational.

4.
Retirement

I N MY 20-SOMETHING brain, a trio of financial ideas came together—the rule of 72, the fact that U.S. stocks had historically outpaced inflation by seven percentage points a year, and the desire to work less hard during the second half of my career.

The rule of 72 says that, if you divide 72 by your rate of return, you can find out how many years it'll take to double your money. If stocks did indeed notch seven percentage points a year more than inflation, the spending power of money invested in the stock market would double after ten years and quadruple after 20 years. My thought: If I could amass $250,000 by age 45 and then leave that money to ride until age 65, I'd have an inflation-adjusted $1 million upon retirement. In the meantime, I could spend the final two decades of my career working part time, with no need to sock away any more money for retirement.

All this, of course, was absurdly naïve. It ignored issues like paying for my kids' college costs, whether historical market returns were predictive and whether $1 million was enough for a comfortable retirement. But perhaps the biggest issue I overlooked was this: Was working less hard, and eventually not working at all, what I really wanted?

For many, the answer would be yes. But retirement wasn't for me. I had the good fortune to love what I did for a living, and found I had no desire to quit entirely. I believe that engaging in meaningful work is one of the three pillars of a happy life, along with a sense of security and a robust network of friends and family. As my life's end approached, I worked somewhat less hard. But I never stopped writing until I had to.

Retire is a Verb

We like to escape the northeast's cold each winter and, on one such trip, we spent ten days in Sarasota, Florida. Like many others when they're on vacation, Elaine and I found our noses pressed against the windows of real-estate offices, perusing the listings and musing about whether we'd want to live there.

Fantasizing about the future is fun and free, but it can also be dangerous. It's how folks end up buying timeshares and second homes during wonderfully relaxing vacations. But vacation, of course, isn't real life. When you live somewhere, what seems special quickly becomes unremarkable. You stop noticing how cute Main Street is—because you're hustling to get to the grocery store before the after-work crowd.

This is also the reason I'm skeptical of those lists of the best places to retire, which are often built around a quantitative assessment of things like crime, tax burden, weather, medical care and so on. Yes, those are important issues. But I don't think they're the keys to a happy retirement.

So, what should we focus on? I'd zero in on three factors—the same three factors that I think are crucial to happiness for everybody, retired or not.

1. Purpose

We won't spend our retirement simply being. Instead, we'll be doing. But what will we do each day that'll make our retirement meaningful and fulfilling? That notion got me to thinking about categories of doing: exercise, hobbies, learning, reading, writing, chores, watching TV, volunteering, worship, working part time, socializing, cooking, eating out, live entertainment, visiting museums, travel and so on.

Some of these activities—chores, reading, writing, worship, watching TV, cooking—can occupy our time no matter where we live. Location doesn't much matter. But others depend on the community we're in. How many theaters, museums and live music venues are nearby? How many decent restaurants? If we want to get outside and exercise, what are our choices? How close are the nearest airport and train station?

Each of us will have a different list of activities we want to engage in. But the crucial thing is to focus on the doing, not the being. We won't be happy for long simply sitting on the deck and admiring the gorgeous view.

2. Friends and family

Next, there's the all-important issue of social connections. We may not want to see others every day. But there's great joy in spending an occasional evening with family and friends.

Will that be possible wherever we choose to retire? If we head to parts unknown, we'll likely make friends—eventually. But it's worth pondering how easy we find it to make new acquaintances, and how easy it'll be for family and old friends to visit.

And, of course, there will likely be a time when our physical or cognitive deterioration demands help from others. That help can be purchased. But it'll be a lot cheaper and probably more pleasant if at least some of that help comes from those we love.

3. Financial contentment

I think money—if used thoughtfully—can buy happiness, though I don't think it can garner as much happiness as, say, a great night's sleep or an hour spent at the playground with a grandchild. Good health and social connections are so much more important to happiness than money.

Instead, I believe money is most useful in helping us to avoid worry, especially worries about not having enough money. Yes, that's the great irony of money: We should accumulate it mostly so we don't have to think about it.

What does that mean for retirement? I think there are two key implications. First, we should organize our financial life with an eye to minimizing money concerns. That might mean downsizing to a less expensive home so we have ample breathing room in our monthly budget. It might also mean delaying Social Security, buying income annuities and holding plenty of cash so our monthly income is less dependent on the vagaries of the financial markets.

Second, if we move in retirement, we shouldn't move to an area where we're surrounded by far wealthier neighbors. Even if we have more than enough money for a comfortable retirement, we may find ourselves comparing our lifestyle to those around us—and suffering a gnawing sense of dissatisfaction.

Buying Freedom

If 20-somethings ask me for financial advice, I suggest getting a job right out of college and saving like crazy, so they quickly get themselves on the fast track to financial freedom.

If 60-somethings ask me for advice, I advocate a phased retirement, seeking part-time work in their initial retirement years and, if they enjoy it, perhaps keeping it up into their 70s.

Yeah, I know, I sound like a real killjoy. My advice raises an obvious question: Is there ever a time when we should cut ourselves some slack and not have a job?

Let me start with this: If you have a burning passion—perhaps to establish yourself as an artist in your 20s or to commit yourself to religious study in your 60s—you already know what you need for a fulfilling life. Everybody else's opinion, including mine, is of little import.

But what if you don't have a calling? It's worth keeping five key ideas in mind:

First, in crass economic terms, adult life is about using our human capital—our income-earning ability—to amass financial capital, so one day we no longer need to rely on our human capital. This "no longer relying on our human capital" is what non-economists call retirement, and it often takes three or four decades of saving and investing to accumulate enough.

Second, beyond paying for retirement and other goals, it's desirable to amass money because it provides a sense of financial security and it gives us the flexibility to lead our life as we wish. If we sock away a moderate amount of savings early on, we'll remove one of life's biggest stressors.

Third, most of us aren't very good at anticipating what our future self will want. Maybe our greatest desire will be to retire early. Perhaps, in our 40s or 50s, we'll want to swap into a career that's less lucrative but more fulfilling. Or maybe we'll be happy to persevere with our current job. It's hard to know what we'll want, which is another reason to save diligently starting early in adult life. The larger our nest egg, the more options we'll have.

Fourth, our focus often shifts as we grow older. We become less motivated by the prospect of pay raises and promotions, and more focused on doing what we personally care about. With any luck, once we have a better handle on what we really want, we'll get the chance to pursue those passions more fully during a second career or once we're retired.

Finally, most of us enjoy striving toward our goals. To be sure, we imagine that the greatest happiness will lie in achieving those goals. But in truth, it's the striving that offers the great pleasure. This pleasure is captured by the notion of flow, those times when we're engaged in activities that we're passionate about, we find challenging, we think are important and we feel we're good at. At such moments, we can become totally absorbed and lose all sense of time. We should design our life—including our retirement—so we enjoy frequent moments of flow.

The five ideas above help explain why we should save early in life to prepare ourselves for later, when we might want to change how we spend our days. But that still leaves one question unanswered: Why, come retirement, should our days necessarily involve working part time?

The short answer is, it isn't necessary. Unless you don't have enough saved, there's no need to work part time in retirement. But I think it's an idea that deserves more attention. Today, retiring as early as possible is considered a badge of honor, and continuing to work later in life is viewed as somehow offensive to the whole notion of retirement.

But there are all kinds of reasons—financial and otherwise—to continue earning money through our 60s and into our 70s. It can feel good to be a productive member of society, plus retirement can be a whole lot less financially stressful if we still have a little money coming in. What about those savings we earlier amassed? Even if we keep earning money, we'll likely still find plenty of uses for our savings, including travel, helping family members, supporting our favorite charities and perhaps paying long-term-care costs.

I'm not saying that working part time in retirement is the right choice for everybody. But if there are activities you find fulfilling, and you can make a little money doing them, why not?

Second Childhood

In college, I was the kid who swore he would never get married and never have children. A year later, I was engaged. Two years later, I was married. Three years later, I had a newborn.

I have no regrets about having children so young. Far from it. It does mean I missed out on the romancing, bar-hopping, commitment-free years that many in their 20s enjoy. But in return for that sacrifice, I had my reward starting at age 51—a period I've come to think of as my second childhood.

Because I was thrust so quickly into the adult world, I was compelled to get serious about money at a relatively early age. I paid off my credit card debt from college, started saving regularly for retirement, bought a house, took on freelance work whenever I could, wrote books at the weekend, and began socking away money for my own children's college.

By 51, my two kids had their bachelor's, my nest egg was large enough for a comfortable retirement and I had lost all enthusiasm for my job at Citigroup, so I quit.

Having done that, I thought of myself as semi-retired: My various ventures earned me far less than what I made as director of financial education for Citi's U.S. wealth management business and, indeed, I found myself spending modestly more than I earned.

Yet, since quitting Citi, I have never worked harder. I've tackled all manner of projects. In addition to launching HumbleDollar, I have authored four books, joined the investment committee and advisory board of Creative Planning, given speeches, worked on a concept for a personal finance app, consulted for Wall Street firms, taught a college course on personal finance for two semesters, written a regular column for first *The Wall Street Journal* and then *Financial Planning* magazine, and penned freelance articles.

When I left Citi, I didn't expect to be so busy, but I have no regrets. I have viewed the time since as my chance to try new things without worrying about what they paid me, and I've wanted to make the most of the opportunity.

What have I learned along the way? Five lessons come to mind—and I think they have implications for others venturing into retirement or semi-retirement.

1. It's hard to know what will make you happy. I enjoy giving speeches and talking to folks about their finances, so I figured I'd love teaching. I was wrong. I expected great things of my students, but most seemed to expect very little of themselves—and I had neither the patience nor the teaching skills needed to bridge that gap.

2. There's great pleasure in working hard at something you're passionate about. I have the financial wherewithal to ditch my various projects and retreat to the couch, but I have no desire to do that. Even in my semi-retirement, I get enormous satisfaction from wrestling with financial questions and writing projects.

3. I wish it were otherwise, but I find it isn't quite enough to help others and do work I consider important. I still enjoy the extra validation that comes with making money and hearing applause. These things aren't as important to me as they once were, but I can't shake them entirely.

4. When you're always home, it's hard to leave it all behind. Entire days can pass without me going outside, especially during winter. My laptop offers seductively easy access to work and to the larger world, and life's necessities—food, booze, toothpaste and toilet paper—can all be delivered.

Problem is, remaining rooted in one spot makes it difficult to escape worries and work pressures. I have been trying to get out more, if only for a brief walk, but I'm not as good about it as I should be.

5. The markets look riskier when you aren't regularly adding new savings to your portfolio. I have always invested heavily in the stock market, and still do. But now that I'm more likely to pull money from my portfolio than add to it, I'm less sanguine about the possibility of a large stock market decline.

As a gut check, I use the strategy I recommend to others: Occasionally, I will take my portfolio and assume the stock portion loses 35%, which is the typical decline during a bear market. I'll then look at the resulting hit to my overall portfolio's value and ask myself, "Would I be okay with that?" If you find yourself fretting about a market decline, try this exercise yourself

Fire Meets Ice

Have we got it all wrong? "It" is our relentless, lifelong focus on socking away great wads of money, so we don't have to worry about earning another penny once we reach our 60s.

In fact, adherents of the FIRE—financial independence, retire early—movement aim to reach this blissful state far earlier, perhaps even in their 30s. This, of course, involves saving voraciously, with all the financial sacrifice that's entailed. Even retiring in our 60s can seem like a Herculean task, generating much hand-wringing and financial stress. Is all this really necessary?

For those less enthralled with the traditional vision of retirement or its more extreme FIRE version, let me suggest an alternative. I've dubbed it ICE, short for "I'll continue earning."

Ponder two questions. First, are we overly focused on amassing ungodly sums for retirement? Second, should we strive to remain useful throughout our life, rather than bowing out of the workforce in our 60s or earlier?

I think our current concept of retirement could do with some tweaking. I wouldn't want to discourage folks from saving aggressively for their later years. At the same time, it's instructive to think about a different model of retirement, one where we continue to earn at least some income well into our 70s and perhaps beyond. Consider five implications:

1. From the get-go, we might pick a career less for its income and more for its joy—because we envisage doing it for as long as our

mind and body allow. As the saying goes, if we can find a job we love, we'll never work a day in our life.

2. All the anxiety over saving like crazy and investing prudently would be much diminished, because the financial stakes would be far lower. Sure, we'd still need to save for house down payments, college costs, financial emergencies and some period at the end of our life when we're no longer able to do the work we love. But the total sum involved would be far smaller, and meeting all these goals would no longer seem like an all-but-impossible financial juggling act.

3. Similarly, all the fretting over finding the right retirement-income strategy would be greatly reduced. To state the obvious, retirement's fundamental financial dilemma is we're trying to pay for decades of living expenses without a paycheck coming in. With the ICE model, this problem is largely solved: Our "retirement" income might consist of Social Security, a paycheck and—if that paycheck is smaller because we're working part time—some modest amount of savings. The math is compelling: If we can earn $30,000 a year with part-time work, that's like having a nest egg that's $750,000 larger, assuming a 4% withdrawal rate.

4. Today's pressing demographic problem—too few workers, and too many folks dependent on the goods and services that they provide—would be solved. That, in turn, would mean less reliance on imported goods and hence a smaller trade deficit, less inflationary pressure, fewer labor shortages and more taxes collected, including the payroll taxes needed to keep Social Security on a sound financial footing.

5. The whole issue of finding a purpose in retirement goes away. Our work remains our purpose. And thanks to the physical, social and intellectual stimulation that this work provides, we'd likely enjoy longer, healthier lives.

Among readers, I can imagine two big objections to all this. First, what if we simply can't work, because either our mind or body won't allow it? Wouldn't we need a huge pile of savings for that? No doubt about it, this is a big issue, one we all potentially face, as evidenced by the many families that struggle today to provide and pay for long-term care. The bottom line: Even if we hope to keep working, we need to be financially prepared if that hope doesn't pan out.

Second, what if we really want that life of endless leisure? Or what if we want to spend our later years doing things that nobody's likely to pay us to do, such as writing poetry or volunteering at our place of worship? Clearly, the ICE strategy doesn't work.

Still, I'd contend our current retirement ideal—that the good life means stopping all paid work in our 60s and perhaps earlier—rests on two questionable assumptions: that work is a distasteful task that we should escape as soon as we can, and that our goal should be to spend our later years avoiding anything so useful to society that it comes with a paycheck.

I realize that many, and perhaps most, folks have bought into these two assumptions. But wouldn't it be great if we viewed work and retirement differently? Indeed, I suspect that, if they could do work that they love on a flexible schedule, a lot of retirees would jump at the chance to enjoy the income, camaraderie, and sense of identity and purpose that work can offer.

Convinced? Even as I advance these ideas, I must confess to cold feet. If my younger self hadn't saved like crazy for retirement and I now faced the prospect of working for the rest of my life, would I feel happy with my choice—or trapped? Can any of us reliably predict in our 30s what our desires will be in our 60s?

Still, I think there's an opportunity here for each of us individually and for us as a society. Businesses, faced with ongoing labor shortages, should be working to design jobs that would appeal to older citizens. We should be tweaking the tax code to make it more financially attractive for seniors to keep working, knowing the revenue that the government gives up would be more than offset by the additional taxes that these older workers end up paying.

And we should all be thinking not just about saving enough for retirement, but also about what work we'd love to do in retirement and how we could get paid for doing it. If we can identify that perfect job, maybe our 60s and 70s would be a whole lot less financially stressful—and a whole lot more fulfilling.

5.
Lists

J OURNALISM ALWAYS SEEMED like a possible career path for me. My father was a financial journalist for his first ten years in the workforce, working in London for the *Financial Times*, *The Glasgow Herald* and *The Daily Telegraph*, and I grew up hearing his stories of life as an ink-stained wretch.

My start in journalism was more modest. I got my first full-time job at age 19, working for a tiny newspaper in the Maryland suburbs of Washington, D.C. I had nine months between leaving boarding school and starting at Cambridge, and I spent most of that time at the paper, covering sports, education, police and whatever else came my way. It was a wonderful introduction to journalism, and I had a blast, soaking up the wisdom passed along by the newspaper's staff.

Still, in the years that followed, I came to realize that I simply wasn't that good a reporter. I never enjoyed picking up the phone, calling strangers and asking tough questions. I've never been keen on confrontation, probably a legacy of boarding school and the bullying I endured. I much preferred researching financial issues and coming up with my own take.

I got lucky.

In 1994, *The Wall Street Journal* Managing Editor Paul Steiger announced that the newspaper would be interested in adding three columnists to the paper's news pages (as opposed to the editorial pages, which operated as a separate department and had long had columnists). I put up my hand and, at the absurdly young age of 31, was given one of the three columnist slots.

The column, dubbed "Getting Going," evolved over the years as my financial interests changed. But one feature was a constant:

lists. As I discovered early on, readers love lists, and it became a go-to format for my columns. A list of ten items was often popular. But to catch readers' attention, an odd number often proved even more compelling. "Seven things to do now" sounded a whole lot more intriguing than "six steps to take today."

My enthusiasm for the list format has waned somewhat over the years. Nonetheless, as you'll see in this chapter, I continued to make frequent use of numbered lists for my HumbleDollar articles.

Nobody Told Me

I have devoted my adult life to learning about money. That might sound like cruel and unusual punishment, but I've mostly enjoyed it. For more than three decades, I've spent my days perusing the business pages, reading finance books, scanning academic studies and talking to countless folks about their finances.

Yet, despite this intense education, it took me a decade or more to learn many of life's most important money lessons and, indeed, some key insights have only come to me in recent years. Here are ten things I wish I'd been told in my 20s—or told more loudly, so I actually listened.

1. A small home is the key to a big portfolio. My first wife and I bought a modest house because we worried that we couldn't afford anything bigger. I ended up living in that house for two decades.

   Financially, it turned out to be one of the smartest things I've ever done, because it allowed me to save great gobs of money. That's clear to me in retrospect. But I wish I'd known it was a smart move at the time, so I didn't waste so many hours wondering whether I should have bought a larger place.

2. Debts are negative bonds. From my first month as a homeowner, I sent in extra money with my mortgage payment, so I could pay off the loan more quickly. But it was only later that I came to view my mortgage as a negative bond—one that was costing me dearly. In fact, paying off debt almost always garners a higher after-tax return than you can earn by investing in high-quality bonds.

3. Watching the market and your portfolio doesn't improve performance. This has been another huge time waster. It's a bad habit I'm belatedly trying to break.

4. Thirty years from now, you'll wish you'd invested more in stocks. Yes, over five or even ten years, there's some chance you'll lose money in the stock market. But over 30 years? It's highly likely you'll notch handsome gains, especially if you're broadly diversified and regularly adding new money to your portfolio in good times and bad.

5. Nobody knows squat about short-term investment performance. This is closely related to point No. 4. One of the downsides of following the financial news—or, worse still, working as a columnist at *The Wall Street Journal*—is that you hear all kinds of smart, articulate experts offering eloquent predictions of plummeting share prices and skyrocketing interest rates that—needless to say—turn out to be hopelessly, pathetically wrong. In my early days as an investor, this was, alas, the sort of garbage that would give me pause.

6. Put retirement first. When I was in my 20s, I remember a financial expert saying, "If you don't own a house by age 30, you'll likely never own one." I didn't realize it at the time, but not only was this alarmist nonsense, but also it prioritized the wrong thing.

   Buying a house shouldn't be our top goal. Instead, retirement should be. It's so expensive to retire that, if you don't save at least a modest sum in your 20s, the math quickly becomes awfully tough—and you'll need a huge savings rate to amass the nest egg you need.

7. You'll end up treasuring almost nothing you buy. Over the years, I've had fleeting desires for all kinds of material goods. Sometimes, I caved in and bought. Most of the stuff I purchased has since been thrown away.

Today, I have a handful of paintings and some antique furniture that I prize, and that's about it. This is an area where millennials seem far wiser than us baby boomers. They're much more focused on experiences than possessions—a wise use of money, says happiness research.

8. Work is so much more enjoyable when you work for yourself. These days, I earn just a fraction of what I made during my six years on Wall Street, but I'm having so much more fun. No meetings to attend. No employee reviews. No worries about getting to the office on time or leaving too early. I'm working harder today than I ever have. But it doesn't feel like work—because it's my choice and it's work that I'm passionate about.

9. Will our future self approve? As we make decisions today, I think this is a hugely powerful question to ask—and yet it's only in recent years that I've learned to ask it.

   When we opt not to save today, we're expecting our future self to make up the shortfall. When we take on debt, we're expecting our future self to repay the money borrowed. When we buy things today of lasting value, we're expecting our future self to like what we purchase.

   Pondering our future self doesn't just improve financial decisions. It can also help us to make smarter choices about eating, drinking, exercising and more. Tempted to have one more slice of pizza? Tomorrow's self would likely prefer you didn't.

10. Relax, things will work out. As I watch my son, daughter and their spouses wrestle with early adult life, I glimpse some of the anxiety that I suffered in my 20s and 30s.

    When you're starting out, there's so much uncertainty—what sort of career you'll have, how financial markets will perform, what misfortunes will befall you. And there will be misfortunes. I've had my fair share.

But if you regularly take the right steps—work hard, save part of every paycheck, resist the siren song of get-rich-quick schemes—good things should happen. It isn't guaranteed. But it's highly likely. So, for goodness' sake, fret less about the distant future, and focus more on doing the right things each and every day.

Never Assume

Throughout the day, we make countless snap judgments, often without realizing it. Think about navigating the grocery store. This involves a blizzard of decisions—which brand, what size, whether it's good value, will it stay fresh—and yet we do so almost effortlessly.

Most of the time, this is a good thing. If we carefully pondered the assumptions behind every judgment we make, life would become painfully unproductive. Still, it's helpful occasionally to question whether we're misjudging the world, especially when it comes to money issues. Examples? Here are 35 assumptions we shouldn't make:

1. People who are richer are happier.
2. A fund's past performance will repeat.
3. Other points of view are without merit.
4. Endless relaxation is what we really want.
5. Stock market investors—in aggregate—care greatly about anything other than interest rates and future corporate earnings.
6. Our future self won't regret the money we're merrily spending today.
7. Great companies will be great stocks.
8. An insurance agent is selling us the best investment products for our financial future.
9. An item on sale is a bargain.
10. Our immediate reaction is the right one.
11. Sophisticated investment products and strategies deliver better returns.
12. Paying less in taxes is always financially smart.

13. Silence means someone agrees with us.

14. The collective judgment of investors, as reflected in market prices, is wrong.

15. People who claim to beat the market actually have.

16. We'll have the same high tolerance for risk when share prices are 30% lower.

17. We're being rational.

18. Investment experts pontificating on TV have any clue what will happen next in the economy and the financial markets.

19. Friends and family are telling us the unvarnished truth.

20. Material progress—the bigger house, the faster car, the next pay raise—will deliver lasting happiness.

21. A fee-only financial advisor has no conflicts of interest.

22. Financial reporters fully understand what they're talking or writing about.

23. How we think we're perceived is how we're perceived.

24. Those who are most insistent or passionate are most likely to be correct.

25. Extraordinary career and investment success is all about talent and hard work—and that luck plays no role.

26. Last year's insurance coverage still fits our circumstances today.

27. High investment costs are an indication we're getting something special.

28. Our home will be a great investment.

29. We instinctively know what will make us happy.

30. Our life in the years ahead will be similar to today.

31. We know something other investors don't.

32. People who appear wealthy actually are wealthy.

33. Our recollection is correct.

34. Our thinking isn't swayed by the investment mob's euphoria and despair.

35. When the job is finally done, we'll feel a lasting sense of triumph.

Advice for the Kids

When Hannah and Henry were children, I talked a lot about money. This was partly self-preservation: It would have been embarrassing if the kids of a personal-finance columnist grew up to be financial ne'er-do-wells.

Fortunately, they didn't. Hannah and Henry are now in their 30s. Both have good financial habits, and today I typically don't talk to them about money except when they have questions. Still, given my cancer diagnosis, perhaps a few final reminders are in order—13, to be precise:

1. Be an optimist

When you buy bonds, you rent out your money and get interest in return. But when you purchase stocks, you become an owner—and owning is the road to wealth. Sure, if the global economy collapses, you'll end up broke. But so will everybody else, including those conservative folks who spent their life cowering in bonds and cash investments.

Moreover, over the long haul, losing money with a diversified stock portfolio strikes me as unlikely. Every morning, billions of people around the world wake up, trying to figure out how they can make their life better. Buying stocks is a way to profit from that energy and dynamism.

2. Don't pay too much attention

By this, I mean don't look at your portfolio too often, don't listen to market pundits and don't fiddle with your investment mix. If I'd done that from the get-go, I would have saved myself a lot of time—and you'd be inheriting a lot more money.

3. Own the world

Buy the Vanguard Total World Stock Index, which owns every stock of any consequence, and then let your money ride. Which will shine, U.S. or foreign stocks, growth or value, large or small? With a total world fund, there's no need to guess. As long as the global economy keeps growing, so will your portfolio.

4. Use your superpower

Are the talking heads prattling on about a possible market crash? That might be unnerving if you plan to spend all your savings in the next few years. Otherwise, ignore such nonsense. Instead, think and act like a truly long-term investor—something even most professional money managers fail to do, because they're worried about their year-end bonus and about losing clients. The ability to play the long game is the everyday investor's superpower, but one that's all too rarely used.

5. Buy more when stocks drop sharply

Whenever the stock market tumbles, folks offer reasons the decline will get worse. They'll point to high valuations, or geopolitical concerns, or a potentially vicious economic contraction. But we've seen this movie numerous times.

Over my investing career, whenever stocks have plunged, I've instinctively bought more, backed by my confidence that the world economy will keep growing and that my globally diversified stock portfolio will benefit from the eventual recovery. This has been one of the biggest contributors to my portfolio's growth, along with indexing and a voracious savings habit.

6. Unburden yourself

There's plenty of debate over whether it's smart to pay off mortgages and other borrowed money faster than required, and yet I've never heard anyone say, "I wish I wasn't debt-free." Paying off debt earns you a guaranteed return equal to the loan's interest rate—and that rate is typically higher than you could earn by buying bonds and cash investments.

7. Play soft defense

Insurers and their salespeople will happily sell you blanket coverage— but that's an expensive proposition. What to do? Favor policies with high deductibles and long elimination periods. Ditch those that become superfluous, such as life and disability insurance after you've amassed enough for retirement. Also, for your emergency fund, aim for three months of living expenses, rather than the recommended six. You don't want to leave too much of your wealth languishing in cash.

8. Have each other's back

None of us wants to ask family members for money if we find ourselves out of work or facing unexpectedly large bills. But it's good to know that last resort exists. Be each other's safety net, making it clear you stand ready to help if things get rough.

9. Great happiness comes from the money you don't spend

I'm not saying you shouldn't treat yourself occasionally to dinners out, coveted possessions and special vacations. But if you want to buy long-term happiness, also strive for the sense of financial security that comes from a plump portfolio. It's the one purchase you'll never regret.

10. Travel lightly

We end up amassing countless possessions that quickly lose their allure. Do yourself a favor: Ruthlessly shed items you don't need and don't care about. I've dumped all manner of possessions over the past dozen years, and not once have I hankered to have any of them back.

11. Humans are hard-wired to worry

Blame this on our loss aversion, which isn't just about money. Everywhere we turn, we see the possibility that we'll be on life's losing end, and yet most of the time things turn out fine. My advice: Be aware of risk—but don't go into full-worry mode unless it's truly warranted.

For instance, I've read that 10% of folks have no problem afflicting harm on others, while the other 90% aim to do good. I have no idea whether these estimates are accurate, but they seem reasonable. You should, of course, be alert for the malicious 10%. But I'd encourage you to assume that most folks—colleagues, neighbors, chance acquaintances—have good intentions.

To that end, don't read too much into texts and emails, especially those from colleagues. Most people aren't artful in their use of language, so their intent may be muddied, and things will likely be even worse if you try to read between the lines. Instead, until people prove themselves untrustworthy, give them the benefit of the doubt. That attitude will make the world seem like a more pleasant place, and you'll spend far less time fretting unnecessarily.

12. Aim for a sense of accomplishment

Want to feel content? Strive to achieve one or two key goals each day, and you'll likely reach evening feeling tired but fulfilled.

13. Pay it forward

Make sure your children grow up with sound financial values. Push them to get good educations. Help Martin, Teddy and any future children to launch their financial life. Guide their money choices. Don't just talk the talk—also model good financial behavior.

Granny and Grandpa did that for me, and I've endeavored to do that for you. We aren't a wealthy family. But we can strive to lift up each generation that follows, so our family remains financially resilient—and doesn't suffer the suffocating money stress that afflicts so many.

Got to Believe

As I've built out HumbleDollar, I've come to view the site not merely as a place where folks can learn about financial issues, but as a community that thinks about money in a unique way.

This shows up repeatedly in contributors' articles, with their focus on topics like spending thoughtfully, helping family, behavioral finance, indexing and achieving financial freedom. It's a community where folks are trying to be rational about money, but are also acutely aware of the human dimension.

That got me thinking that HumbleDollar ought to have a manifesto—key principles that should govern how we use and think about money. Here are a dozen initial principles:

1. Our financial life involves endless trade-offs. We usually have a good idea of what our dollars are buying us. But to be good stewards of our wealth, we should also ponder what we're giving up.
2. It takes years to achieve full financial freedom. But we can quickly escape much financial worry if we live beneath our means, pay off credit card debt and build a cash cushion.
3. Good savings habits are the greatest of the financial virtues. If we aren't good savers, it's all but impossible to grow wealthy. What if we are? We'll likely prosper, even if we're mediocre investors.
4. We should focus relentlessly on what we want from our financial life. That'll motivate us to save, drive our investment strategy and help ensure we pursue the goals we care about most.

5. Retirement may be our final financial goal, but we should always put it first. Why? It's easily our most expensive goal, so it takes decades of savings and investment gains to amass enough.

6. We spend too much time fretting over our investments—where there's limited room to add value—and too little on other financial issues, like taxes, insurance and estate planning.

7. Paying down debt may not be our best investment, but it's almost never a bad idea. It reduces our life's financial risk and earns us a rate of return equal to the debt's interest rate.

8. Very few of us need life insurance for our entire life. That's why term insurance makes sense and cash-value policies are usually a mistake—despite what insurance agents say.

9. Investing is best when it is simplest. If we own costly, complicated products, we're filling Wall Street's coffers at our own expense. Don't understand an investment? Don't buy it.

10. Our odds of beating the market averages over a lifetime of investing are so small they're hardly worth considering. Overconfident investors insist on trying. Rational investors index.

11. Our goal shouldn't be more time to relax, but rather more time to pursue our passions. Working hard at things we care deeply about is among life's greatest pleasures.

12. Frugality isn't just the key to financial success. It's also no great sacrifice, because spending often brings only fleeting happiness and sometimes even pangs of regret.

Short and Sweet

As I was preparing for HumbleDollar's December 31, 2016, launch, my web developer suggested I add a mission statement to the top of the homepage. That mission statement morphed into a daily insight that also became a daily Tweet. Like the family that moves from a three-bedroom house to a one-bedroom apartment, I embraced the challenge of shoehorning financial ideas into 140 characters or less.

Twitter—now X—has since expanded the allowable character count, but I try to stick to the old 140 limit. Here are 40 of those daily insights:

1. We get just one shot at making the journey from birth to retirement. Flirting with financial disaster is not advisable.
2. If you waste money, you can make more. If you waste time, life gets old really fast.
3. Picking superior investments is a crowded trade. Saving more is an easy win.
4. What's the difference between an equity-indexed annuity and an index fund? One needs an army of salespeople. The other sells itself.
5. Want to feel short? Hang out with people who are tall. Want to feel poor? Hang out with folks who are rich.
6. If your kids can borrow it or your friends can admire it, it doesn't count as an investment.
7. Draw up a list of your greatest pleasures in life. Then ask yourself: Do you need great wealth to enjoy any of them?

8. If your portfolio isn't built around broad market index funds, you've got to ask yourself one question, "Do I feel lucky?" Well, do ya, punk?

9. When you're ill, you realize how great it is to feel healthy. Money's similar: When you're broke, you realize how great it is to be solvent.

10. If you think money managers are overpaid, imagine how much they'd charge if they actually beat the market.

11. You want investments that you boast about when you sell—but you're too nervous to discuss when you buy.

12. A boat is not your financial friend, but a friend with a boat is.

13. If you advocate keeping investing simple and making it understandable, you'll lose half your audience, who assume success lies in their own befuddlement.

14. Never confuse the appearance of affluence with affluence. One is the mortal enemy of the other.

15. We are voracious acquirers of financial information, but mostly to buttress opinions we already hold.

16. A quick way to lose half your wealth: Get divorced. The slower route: Marry someone with bad financial habits.

17. If folks claim their home has been a great investment, ask to see their detailed financial records—and their degree in advanced mathematics.

18. Whenever you open your wallet, you're voting for one thing, but also voting against something else.

19. Invest based on dinner seminars, glossy brochures and TV advertisements, and you foot the bill for your own fleecing.

20. If you think today's purchase will make you happy forever, you need to spend more time looking through your closets.

21. Everybody's a long-term investor when the market is going up.

22. Is it time to have the talk with your kids? You know, the important one—about how much you'll help with college costs.

23. Trying to beat the market is a game for the rich. Only they can afford the inevitable disappointing results.

24. Want to be free of financial worries? That hinges on the size of your bank account—and the magnitude of your wants and anxieties.

25. Cash value life insurance isn't an investment, it's a religion—and you'll never meet a more prickly group of disciples.

26. If you save $5 a day for 40 years by not buying coffee, you'll miss out on an awful lot of caffeine.

27. Overconfident investors trade too much, damaging their returns. But heartened by their brokers' applause, they courageously carry on.

28. Dollar-cost averaging is for wimps. You'd be amazed how many rich wimps there are.

29. Forget this year's stock market angst—and ponder the riches that will accrue to those who can ignore it.

30. Another year passes and still there are no inductees to the market-timing hall of fame.

31. It's hard to know who is less truthful, teenage boys boasting of their sexual conquests—or middle-aged men touting their investment prowess.

32. What would happen if everybody indexed? Seriously? Are we really worried about a global outbreak of financial prudence?

33. Good news is bad news: When markets rally, our portfolios may grow fatter—but future returns will likely be lower.

34. We might retire from the workforce, but we should never retire from the pursuit of a fulfilling life.

35. Gold as a portfolio diversifier is like your crazy uncle at the wedding: He dances wildly—and he dances alone.

36. Your kids will grow up to imitate your financial habits. Will you like what you see?

37. If the answer necessitates making a short-term market prediction, you're asking the wrong question.

38. The results speak for themselves—and that's a problem for active money managers.

39. The big financial risk isn't dying early in retirement but, rather, living longer than we ever imagined.
40. Our only earthly immortality will be the recollection of others. Make sure those memories are good.

6.
Behavior

I WROTE MY FIRST article about behavioral finance in 1995. In those early years as a *Wall Street Journal* columnist, it became one of my go-to topics. The academic research offered fascinating insights into human behavior that was backed by rock-solid data and which could help everyday investors improve their money management.

The research sought to answer the perennial questions: Why don't we save enough for retirement? Why does our attitude toward risk change along with the stock market? Why do we build badly diversified portfolios? Why do we insist on trying to beat the market averages when the data say we're likely to fail badly?

In the decades that followed, I came to realize that our quirky human behavior didn't just infect our investing. It also influenced our spending choices, which were often driven by the memories of youth and by our wish to signal our preferred self-image to others.

In addition, I came to realize how difficult it is to change behavior. It's hard for spenders to become savers—but it's also tough to start spending after a lifetime of frugality. Such struggles aren't just about money. Many folks spend their entire life trying to control their weight, or eat more healthily, or exercise more. Often, they'll briefly succeed, only to revert to earlier, more destructive patterns of behavior.

For decades, I thought of myself as a master of self-discipline. I can tune out distractions, put down my head and work for hours with a scary intensity. I've exercised almost every day for the past 30 years, as I trained to run road races and improve as a cyclist. Indeed, I continued to exercise daily even as my cancer took its toll.

But despite that self-discipline when it comes to work and exercise, I too have my behavioral struggles. I know that, after a rough day,

I'm more likely to console myself with an extra glass of wine or an unhealthy dinner. If we're relying on willpower to keep ourselves on track, behaving well is likely to be a daily struggle—and we'll almost inevitably find ourselves slipping. But when good behavior turns into good habits, we can often stay on the straight and narrow.

Reflect Pause Focus

Want to get more out of your money? Whether you're spending or investing, try this three-pronged strategy:

1. Reflect

There's ample evidence that most of us aren't good at investing or at figuring out what will make us happy. Looking to improve? Spend a little time pondering the past.

When during your life were you happiest—and what were you doing? This may help you figure out whether you should change careers and what you might do with your spare time or with your retirement. Also think about the money you've spent in recent years. Which expenditures delivered plenty of happiness—and which do you recall with a shrug of the shoulders and maybe even a touch of regret?

Research suggests that spending on experiences delivers more happiness than spending on possessions. One reason: We tend to forget the incidental annoyances of vacations, dinner parties and other experiences, and instead recall the overall good time. By contrast, it's hard to forget the annoyances that accompany possessions, because they stick around and we have to watch them deteriorate.

Recalling past investments is a little more perilous because our recollection may be sanitized, as we remember our successes and conveniently forget our mistakes. In fact, we may not simply forget our mistakes, but recall doing the exact opposite.

We might have two contradictory thoughts. One says, "I believe I'm smart about money." The other says, "I sold stocks at the March

2020 market bottom." To ease our psychological distress, we might conveniently forget our panic selling—and perhaps even decide that we were buyers of stocks in early 2020.

A possible cure: Dive into the filing cabinet and pull out your old account statements. That could be a sobering reminder of all the bum investments you've bought over the years—and all the ill-timed purchases and sales you have made.

2. Pause

I have become increasingly convinced that there's great value in pausing between an initial thought and acting upon it. There are two reasons.

First, it gives us a cooling-off period, during which we can ponder whether we have settled on the right course of action. We've all had snap reactions—for example, to an email from a colleague or family member—that we later regret and which, with a few hours delay, we would have handled differently.

The same holds true for spending and investing decisions. We fall in love with an expensive pair of shoes or a new electronic toy, make the impulse purchase and later wonder whether it was money well spent. The market surges or sinks, we make a change to our portfolio and later wish we hadn't been so hasty.

Moving slowly doesn't just help us avoid mistakes. It can also boost happiness. That brings us to the second reason to pause. It turns out that delaying spending, whether on experiences or possessions, can bring with it a pleasurable period of anticipation. The implication: If you plan to buy a new car or take a special vacation, start thinking about it far in advance, so you have a long time to savor the eventual prize. You may even discover the months of anticipation prove more pleasurable than the car or vacation itself.

3. Focus

When one of my favorite sports teams loses, I don't bother to read the account in the newspaper. Why upset myself further? But when the team wins, I go hunting for the newspaper recap—even if I'd watched the game. In terms of our happiness, what matters is what we focus on.

For instance, research suggests that high-income earners don't enjoy their daily lives any more than the rest of us and yet, when surveyed, they're more likely to say they are happy. Why? When asked about their level of happiness, those with high incomes ponder their fat paychecks—and that prompts them to say they're happy.

This mindset creates a conundrum, even for those with plenty: Unless you're the world's richest individual, there will always be somebody who has more money than you. Don't want to feel relatively deprived? Don't put yourself in a position where you feel poor. That means avoiding high-end stores and restaurants that you can barely afford, and resisting the temptation to move to a town where others are much wealthier.

Even as you avoid thinking about those who have more, you should spend time considering your own good fortune. Remember the expensive kitchen renovation you undertook two years ago—and which today you barely notice? Spend some time admiring your fine kitchen and you'll squeeze a little more happiness out of the dollars spent.

This notion of focus can also help with investing. If an investment is volatile and hence likely to fall hard during declining markets, experts will often describe it as risky. But this risk is much reduced if we don't need to sell during the market decline—and the sense of risk is diminished even further if we don't pay attention.

Indeed, I've heard many folks say they look at their brokerage and mutual fund accounts less often when financial markets are falling. That strikes me as sensible. If you are well diversified, there's no need to torture yourself with frequent reminders that you're now poorer. As a money manager once told me, "If you own growth stocks, you should only look at the price every 12 months. That way, you'll only suffer one sleepless night a year."

Declaring Victory

I often feel like the Grinch, who "puzzled and puzzled 'till his puzzler was sore." One question I've puzzled over endlessly: If what I do barely matters in the greater scheme of things, why in the world do I keep doing it?

Here are four related thoughts that often preoccupy me:

1. One of life's great pleasures is working hard at something we care deeply about.
2. While striving toward our goals can bring great satisfaction, achieving them is often a letdown.
3. We should worry less about the praise of others and more about doing work we find personally meaningful, because only the latter will reliably deliver happiness.
4. Five or ten years after we're gone, most of us will be forgotten, except by friends and family.

We know why we keep pushing forward: It's our hunter-gatherer instincts. We're here today because our nomadic ancestors were never satisfied with what they had and instead—in their efforts to survive—strove relentlessly for more. The feeling of satisfaction we get when we make progress is a trick played on us by our genes, so we keep working hard.

But if we know this, why don't we learn to chill out? Now that our daily existence isn't a life-or-death struggle, doesn't our relentless pursuit of progress start to seem like the frenzied activity of delusional men and women?

This brings us back to the old battle between "more" and "enough." Somebody once joked to me that, no matter how much money folks have, their idea of being rich was having twice as much. But today, I'm not talking about more money or more possessions.

Instead, my focus is on more success—career or otherwise. We keep striving for one more big promotion or one last major achievement, so we can make our mark on the world, go out on a high note and thereafter rest on our laurels. But it almost never works out that way: We slip into retirement and what we achieved is reworked, abandoned, ruined or simply forgotten.

I try to comfort myself with the notion that we're part of a conversation that stretches across the generations. We build on the work of folks who came before us and whose names we most likely don't know. And our work will be built on by those who follow, and they most likely won't know our names, either.

But I also think we should try to figure out what success looks like, so we can finish our life's work with some sense of satisfaction. I've been endeavoring to do this myself. I think of HumbleDollar as my last big project—and I hope to keep it going for as long as possible.

At some point, however, I also want to feel like I've succeeded. But how will I know? I'm pondering what my goal should be—perhaps a target number of monthly website page views—so I'll know when to declare victory and be satisfied with what I've achieved. If you're looking ahead to the end of your career or the end of the more active part of your retirement, I'd encourage you to engage in the same exercise.

Ponder what constitutes success and then write it down, so you don't start moving the goal posts. To be honest, I'm not 100% sure this will work. But maybe, just maybe, if you achieve your written goal, you'll have some peace of mind—and you won't spend your remaining days wishing you had achieved more.

Why We Struggle

I've spent much of my life trying to better understand the world, especially the financial world. But I wonder whether I should have spent more of that time trying to better understand myself.

Why do some financial situations scare us, while others leave us unperturbed? Why do we spend time and money in ways we later regret? Why do we find our bad habits so difficult to change? Why do we admire some folks, while being jealous of others?

These questions are better directed to a psychologist than some aging, ink-stained wretch. Still, it's questions like these that have fascinated me in recent years. I can't claim to have the answers—but I have some sense for why they're difficult to answer.

It takes years to know ourselves

It's embarrassing to think back on the self-confidence of my 20-something self. I was so sure I knew what I wanted and that my way was the right one.

The decades that followed have highlighted how wrong I was. For instance, my instinct is to assume that others have good intentions. While that's usually the case, it isn't always. One consequence: I've occasionally been taken advantage of by folks I considered friends. Fortunately, while the emotional toll has sometimes been large, the financial cost has been modest.

But perhaps the big danger isn't the personality traits about which we have some inkling, but rather aspects of our personality that we're completely clueless about. Others might be able to fill us in on our shortcomings—if we're humble enough to let them.

So much of who we are is innate, and much of the rest reflects early life experiences

There's plenty of advice on what we can do to boost our happiness. But even if we followed all this advice, the impact would likely be modest. Why? We all have a happiness set point—an innate predisposition to be more or less happy—and that has a far bigger impact on whether we tend to be happy or not.

Layered on top of our innate personality traits are our life experiences, especially those from early in our lives. In my 20s, when I was raising two children on a junior reporter's salary and money was in short supply, I remember my panic whenever I was faced with a car or home repair bill. Today, I can easily handle such bills, and yet a major expense can still bring back memories of those panicked moments from four decades ago.

We're bad at figuring out what will make us happy

Why do we often waste money on things that bring us little happiness? Why are our closets and basements full of possessions we regret buying? We think we know what will make us happy, and yet we're frequently wrong. My hunch: We go astray because we often spend money based on the influence of others, both past and present.

Bad habits are extraordinarily hard to break

It's said that good and bad habits compound, and I believe it. My good habits—the discipline to exercise every day and to block out distractions so I can focus on the work I need to get done—have become so much a part of me that I can't imagine changing.

What about my bad habits? That's another matter entirely. For instance, at a restaurant, I'll order an entrée simply because it comes with French fries, even if there's another entrée I prefer—and even though I know I shouldn't be eating fries. I'm especially susceptible to ordering the wrong thing if I've had a rough day and my "willpower budget" is at a low ebb. The good news: At home, Elaine largely dictates what we eat, and her inclinations are far healthier than mine.

Of course, eating isn't our only outlet if we're at a low ebb. Plenty of folks find other damaging ways to cheer themselves up, whether it's spending too much, having a few drinks, buying lottery tickets, or even making a few trades in their portfolio.

Life's randomness is hard to accept

Why do some folks struggle financially their entire life, while others fly up the corporate ladder at fast-growing companies with booming share prices? Often, it's easy to see the role of luck in the suffering and successes of others, so we'd be wise to assume that we, too, aren't fully in control of our own fate.

Focusing on luck may help us to cope with one of life's least admirable emotions: jealousy. When we think about our successes—financial, career and otherwise—we tend to think not in absolute terms, but about how we've done relative to contemporaries, including school friends, neighbors, colleagues and siblings. We're not bothered by Warren Buffett's billions. But we're a little jealous about the college friend who ended up as CEO. Perhaps, however, our friend just had better luck than we did.

Today's worries are almost always a waste of time, and yet we worry constantly

Many readers will be aware of the hedonic treadmill—our tendency to quickly grow dissatisfied with our latest accomplishment or purchase, and to start striving after something new, confident that this new goal will deliver lasting happiness.

We can think about our worries in the same vein. We finally put our latest fear to rest, only to start fretting about something else. It seems we're hard-wired to worry, and the moments when we're completely free of concern are few and far between. This, I assume, was a trait that helped our nomadic ancestors to survive—but I'm not sure it does much for us today, except increasing our unhappiness.

Breaking Bad

We all do things that make us feel good right now, but which aren't so good for us over the long haul. Yes, even me. Yes, even you.

Some of this behavior stems from hard-wired instincts passed down to us from our hunter-gatherer ancestors, like our tendency to consume whenever we can and to focus too much on today, while giving short shrift to tomorrow. Other damaging behavior is the result of habits we've developed, often learned from our parents, that we're now trying to unlearn.

Fighting our instincts and breaking these bad habits is tough. We could try summoning the necessary willpower. But that can be mentally exhausting. It may even backfire, when we decide the effort just expended deserves a reward—and, the next thing we know, we're in the drive-through at McDonald's.

Similarly, knowledge isn't power. We all know we should exercise regularly, eat more fruits and vegetables, and save 10% to 15% of income. But knowing better doesn't mean we'll behave better.

So, how do we change our habits and keep our worst instincts at bay? Consider three steps.

First, know yourself. What causes you to spend too much, eat too much or drink excessively? Do these things tend to happen at a particular time of day, or when you're with certain people, or when you're at certain places, or if you've had a taxing day?

For instance, you might eat too much or eat unhealthily when you go to certain restaurants or if you've had a rough time at work. You might drink too much when you're with certain friends or on Friday evenings. You might shop to feel better if you're despondent. You might trade more when you have CNBC turned on.

Psychologists have identified five key personality traits: agreeableness, conscientiousness, extraversion, neuroticism and openness. Those who display a strong conscientious streak tend to have good financial and other habits. By contrast, those given to neuroticism—the tendency to respond negatively to events—often have a harder time maintaining good habits. If you're in the latter camp, you'll likely find it especially difficult to avoid, say, going on a shopping spree after you've had a tough day.

What to do? That brings us to step No. 2: Make it harder to engage in damaging behavior. Get the potato chips out of the house. Have your regular savings automatically deducted from your paycheck and bank account. Limit the number of times you go to the shopping mall each month. Don't bookmark retail websites on your computer. Delete food delivery apps from your phone. Use a debit card rather than a credit card, so the money comes straight out of your checking account. Alternatively, spend cash only.

Anything that slows us down can potentially nix bad behavior, because straying from the straight and narrow might seem like too much effort. In addition, it gives time for the contemplative side of our brain to wrestle with the instinctual side, and we might decide we don't really need another pair of shoes.

It's also harder to stray if we've told others about the changes we're trying to make. Want to lose ten pounds or go to the gym three times a week? You might find an "accountability partner"—a friend or family member to whom you confide your goals. In addition, you might look for somebody—perhaps the same person—who also wants to lose weight or exercise more, so you have a companion on your self-improvement journey.

Even as you make it harder to engage in bad behavior, you might make it easier to behave well, by using a strategy called "habit stacking." Find something you do regularly, and then add on or incorporate the desired good behavior. Do you leave the office every lunchtime to buy a sandwich? Find a place that's ten minutes' walk farther away, so you get some exercise at the same time.

With any luck, by making it harder to stray and knowing what's likely to trigger bad behavior, you can steer yourself onto the right track. Step No. 3: Keep this good behavior going until it becomes second nature.

Have you heard that it takes 21 days to change your habits? Unfortunately, that notion—which has gained widespread currency and is often asserted as fact—is, in truth, a distorted account of one doctor's observation. A subsequent academic study found that forming new habits can take anywhere from 18 to 254 days.

The key is to find some way to keep ourselves on the right track for that long. A crucial ingredient: positive feedback. When our friends tell us that we look like we're in great shape or they notice we've lost weight, we're encouraged to continue exercising and losing additional pounds.

Similarly, signs of financial progress can encourage us to keep going. I wouldn't focus on your portfolio's value, because a bad market could leave you discouraged and perhaps even unnerved. Instead, I'd focus on the dollar amount you save and see if you can increase that sum each month. Similarly, you might track your monthly credit card bills and strive to charge less than the month before.

If you have a mortgage, you might also add a little to your monthly loan payment, and then watch as both the loan balance and the amount of interest you pay go down. I used to love watching my mortgage balance shrink each month—and that encouraged me to make even larger extra-principal payments.

No, We Can't

Most of us will never be fabulously wealthy and we'll never earn huge incomes. Self-help authors, get-rich-quick seminars and motivational speakers might try to convince us otherwise. But if we turn to these folks for assistance, they're the ones who typically make heaps of money—at our expense.

Such hucksterism doesn't just carry a short-term cost, however. It also causes us to think about our lives in the wrong way, leaving us with an unwarranted sense of failure and distracting us from the right path forward.

Playing our cards

I bristle when I hear people say, "You can be whoever you want to be." That simply isn't true. In my 30s and 40s, I used to run races from one mile through to marathons. I never toed a starting line unless I felt in the best shape possible, or pretty darn close. And yet I could only run so fast. I would have loved to knock off a sub-four-minute mile. But it wasn't on the cards. Not even close. The best I could manage was just below five.

Our physical limitations are easily enumerated. Our other limitations are harder to measure. But they're just as real.

For instance, psychologists believe some of us are simply predisposed to be happier than others. Think about your friends and family, and you'll quickly realize this is true. Similarly, most of us are well aware of our more obvious individual weaknesses. I'm tone deaf, lousy at advanced math and struggle to learn foreign languages.

Fortunately, we also all have strengths. My skills include understanding financial issues and explaining them in plain English. I've been lucky: Society puts an above-average monetary value on the skills I possess.

No doubt, with more hustle, I could turn my particular set of skills into an even bigger paycheck. But there's a limit: I'm never going to make CEO-type money. Still, I'm grateful. I live at a time when my abilities are fairly highly valued. A few hundred years ago, being able to explain complicated financial issues in plain English would likely have qualified me to dig ditches.

The bottom line: Most of us could do a better job with the hand we've been dealt. But we shouldn't fool ourselves. We can't ask for an entirely new hand.

Losing the magic

How can we get more out of the cards we have been dealt? If we can't have a career that earns us great gobs of money, maybe we can amass those gobs by hitting an investment home run.

I've seen plenty of people try to speculate their way to financial success using all kinds of dubious strategies. They day-trade stocks. They buy investments on margin. They bet everything on a few stocks or a single sector of the market. They trade options. They jump in and out of the stock market, trying to catch upswings and sidestep market declines. They hitch their fortunes to some financial guru. They use a boatload of debt to buy a fistful of rental properties.

Underpinning these strategies is the notion that there's a single product or strategy that will answer all our financial prayers. It's out there somewhere. We just need to find it.

But, of course, the search proves futile. There are no magical financial solutions, and yet all too many people spend their entire lives in desperate pursuit.

Finding our answers

The reality: We can't be anybody we want to be and we won't get rich overnight. The possibilities are not limitless. Our lives are not Disney movies. Except in a few rare instances—where success is often built on a modicum of talent and an excess of luck—we will not earn ridiculous amounts of money and we won't end up fabulously wealthy.

That might sound like a downer. But in truth, it's liberating. We can stop hankering after fat paychecks we'll never collect and wealth we'll never accumulate. These things were never in the cards. Maybe more important, they aren't the right yardsticks by which to measure our lives and, if by some slim chance we achieve all that we desire, we would likely be left with a nagging sense of dissatisfaction.

What happens once we put the fanciful nonsense behind us? We free ourselves to focus on getting the most from the money we do have. We can invest to meet our goals, rather than to amass some mythical sum that we imagine will mark us as better people. We can focus on spending our existing dollars wisely, rather than constantly hankering for more. And we can devote our days to doing what we do best, rather than imagining we ought to be doing something else that might be more lucrative—but which we may not enjoy and for which we simply aren't cut out.

Knowing Me

Does our personality help determine our financial success? It seems it does, or so says academic research.

As I mentioned above, psychologists have zeroed in on five key personality traits: extraversion, conscientiousness, agreeableness, neuroticism and openness to experiences. Think of each trait as a spectrum from, say, very conscientious to not at all. Each of us sits somewhere on the five spectrums. Maybe we're a bit of an extravert, somewhat inclined toward neuroticism, and extremely open to new experiences and ideas.

There's a host of websites, some free, where you can take a relatively quick quiz and get scored on the five dimensions. My scores from three free websites were remarkably similar, so taking just one test will likely suffice. What should you make of the five traits?

1. Conscientious individuals are organized and disciplined. They don't leave their clothes on the floor or the dishes in the sink.
2. Openness measures our willingness to embrace new experiences and ideas. Those who score high in this area tend to be more curious and imaginative, while those with low scores are inclined to resist change and new ideas.
3. Agreeable individuals aren't posting snarky comments on the internet. Instead, they're friendly, trusting, upbeat, concerned about others and slow to criticize.
4. Folks who score high on neuroticism aren't necessarily "neurotic" in the colloquial sense. Rather, they struggle with emotions such

as moodiness, sadness, anger and anxiety. At the other end of the spectrum are those who are emotionally stable and even-tempered.
5. Extraverts are the ones you hear talking at parties. They're exactly what you would expect: They're outgoing, sociable and enjoy being the center of attention.

No doubt all of us recognize some of these traits in ourselves and in those around us. But I'd pay particular attention to whichever trait seems to be most pronounced. Understanding who we are—and the mistakes we're inclined to make—won't necessarily prevent us from messing up, but it's clearly a step in the right direction.

What do our key personality trait or traits mean for our career and how we manage money? I pulled insights from a fistful of academic studies. These studies don't always 100% agree with each other, though their findings largely line up. Here's what I learned:

- Neuroticism is linked to less career and financial success, longer periods of unemployment and lower levels of happiness. Meanwhile, more even-tempered individuals tend to have high career earnings, perhaps because these folks are drawn to more stressful, but also more lucrative, occupations.
- Like neuroticism, agreeableness tends to hurt career and financial success. It seems, alas, that nice guys really do finish last. Why? Perhaps those who are most agreeable don't push hard enough to get pay raises, they're too trusting of Wall Street salespeople and they simply don't care enough about amassing money. There's also evidence suggesting that the most agreeable among us tend to borrow too much and save too little.
- Openness to experiences is associated with higher salaries. People who score high on openness may not be as meticulous as those considered conscientious, but perhaps they're more proactive, tackling work tasks with energy and imagination. Openness may

also lead to higher spending, because these folks may be more inclined, say, to go to concerts or to travel.

- Extraversion is associated with higher salaries and greater happiness, no doubt because extraverts are good at building strong connections with colleagues and friends. Extraverts also tend to favor riskier investments. But like those who score high in agreeableness, extraverts tend to borrow too much and save too little, perhaps because they're concerned with outward appearances—the old pitfall of "keeping up with the Joneses."

- Conscientiousness is associated with career and financial success, including lower levels of debt, shorter periods of unemployment and (no surprise here) planning for the future. Indeed, conscientious individuals typically express satisfaction with their life, though they don't seem to be as happy as extraverts. Still, if the goal is a successful, contented financial life, this appears to be the most desirable personality trait.

Indeed, I suspect that those who are conscientious are likely most capable of managing their own money.

What if you're best described by one of the other four traits? You may want to seek out advisors, coaches or mentors to help with your career or your finances, and perhaps both. That said, those who score high in agreeableness should be especially careful about who they turn to for advice. The reason: These folks tend to be too trusting—not always a good idea when dealing with Wall Street.

7.
Happiness

I DISCOVERED HAPPINESS RESEARCH around 2005 or so—which, ironically, was when I wasn't especially happy. I was in my early 40s, stuck in an unhappy relationship and wondering how much longer I could keep cranking out my *Wall Street Journal* column. I soon learned from academic studies that I was hardly alone: Happiness through life tends to be U-shaped, and many people struggle in their 40s.

Happiness research also had a big influence on my thinking half-a-dozen years later, when I put my New Jersey home on the market and bought an apartment on Roosevelt Island, in the middle of New York City's East River. The research says commuting is terrible for happiness, and the move allowed me to cut my trek to the office from 90 minutes to 20.

The research was again on my mind when, in 2014, I quit my job at Citigroup—along with the largest paycheck I ever had—and decided to work for myself. For my entire career, I'd done work I was passionate about. Those six years at Citigroup were the exception, and I realized a ballooning bank account was no compensation for a miserable work life.

Like everybody else, I've had rough times. My first wife demanded a divorce in 1998, and my second wife did the same in 2019. Both were grueling periods, though not as grueling as 2009, when my 75-year-old father was struck and killed by a car while riding his bicycle.

Still, I feel like I've been lucky. For many, happiness is a lifelong struggle, but not for me. The researchers talk about a happiness "set point," our innate tendency to be more or less happy. It seems I have the good fortune to be happy by nature. There's nothing I did to deserve this, but it's a quality that's made it easier to cope with life's setbacks and to enjoy the good times.

You can boost your happiness beyond that set point by, say, seeing friends regularly, spending on experiences rather than possessions, keeping your commute short and getting yourself in good financial shape. But even with all that, your set point will likely be the biggest driver of your happiness.

15 Ways to Happy

We don't pursue money just to put food on the table and a roof over our head. Instead, the hope is to enhance our life. On that score, it seems we aren't doing terribly well: The reported level of happiness in the U.S. is no higher than it was half a century ago.

Could we do better? I believe so. There's been extensive research on happiness in recent decades. Want the Reader's Digest version? These 15 steps could help your happiness:

1. Build wealth

Those with more income and greater wealth typically report higher levels of happiness, though there remains much debate about the precise relationship. Does the impact of money on happiness cap out at some income level? Does more money really improve day-to-day happiness—or only when we think about our standing relative to others? Whatever the case, money seems to help, so go ahead and save a little more. Your future self will thank you.

2. Avoid comparisons

While those with great wealth may get a warm glow when they ponder their bank balance, the rest of us need to tread more carefully: We may feel discontent with our lot in life if we know others have more. This is a reason to avoid living in a town where we'll have rich neighbors, to skip restaurants we can't really afford and to steer clear of salary discussions at the office.

3. Invest in friendship

Regularly seeing friends can give a big boost to happiness. Similarly, marriage seems to be a plus for happiness. But it appears divorce also helps, while widowhood can be devastating.

4. Get religion

Those who are religious tend to report higher levels of happiness, though the connection seems to be strongest among those with lower incomes or who live in less prosperous countries.

5. Work on your health

There's some evidence that we adapt, at least in part, to debilitating medical conditions. Still, those in good health often report higher levels of happiness. Indeed, it appears to be a virtuous circle: Healthier people are happier—and happier people are more likely to take care of their health.

6. Pursue your passions

We get great pleasure from working hard at something we're passionate about and that we feel is important, whether it's at home, in the community or at the office. The pleasure lies less in achieving our goals and more in making progress toward them. Again, there seems to be a virtuous circle: Fulfilling work can boost happiness—and happy workers tend to be more productive.

7. Favor experiences over possessions

This is perhaps the insight from happiness research that's received the greatest attention. But even if we should devote more dollars to experiences, we all end up purchasing some possessions. The key: Think twice about possessions that'll involve ongoing hassles. We're talking about things like the big yard and the second home, both of which can involve substantial maintenance. Meanwhile, we should favor possessions that help us to socialize and to have fun experiences—which, of course, might lead us to conclude that the big yard and the second home aren't so bad.

8. Pay to avoid distasteful tasks

Rather than trying to buy happiness, we might spend money to avoid unhappiness. Don't like cleaning the house or mowing the lawn? We should consider hiring somebody to do these things for us.

9. Cut your commute

We like to feel in control, but that's tough to do if we have a long commute, with the potential for traffic jams, roadworks, and delayed trains and buses. Want to boost happiness? Try moving closer to work.

10. Give back

We tend to think we'll get greater happiness from spending on ourselves, rather than on others. But research suggests otherwise. We should be generous with friends and family, give regularly to charity and also give our time, by volunteering to help causes that we think are important.

11. Make smaller purchases

Just because something costs ten times more doesn't mean we'll get ten times the happiness. The lesson: We'll likely get greater happiness from many small purchases, rather than one big one.

12. Plan ahead

Often, the best part of a purchase or experience is the anticipation, as we look forward to having the kitchen remodeled or getting away for a week. Want more happiness from these expenditures? Make plans far ahead of time.

13. Focus on the positive

I know, I know, this sounds like some cliché from a self-help book. But in terms of our happiness, what matters is what we focus on—so we should strive to ignore irritations and instead zero in on the good parts of each day.

14. Express gratitude

We often quickly adapt to material improvements, while also forgetting the fun experiences we've had. To counteract this tendency, we should pause occasionally to think about the friends and family who surround us, the possessions we've accumulated and the wonderful experiences we've enjoyed.

15. Minimize money worries

Money has the potential to buy happiness. But if we spend recklessly and end up financially stressed, our efforts will likely backfire. Indeed, it seems that—if we pay ahead of time—we often enjoy experiences more, because we aren't thinking about the cost. This notion also applies to retirement: Those with predictable income that covers much of their living costs, whether it's from a pension, Social Security, immediate annuities or elsewhere, appear to have happier retirements.

What doesn't make the above list? Children. I mention this reluctantly, because it'll probably get me hate mail. But the research suggests that raising children doesn't help happiness. Obviously, we're biologically wired to want children—and, once we have adult children and then grandchildren, our growing family can be a source of great joy. But getting there can be rough.

Unhappy Results

Happiness research fascinates me—and I'm not alone. Many of the insights uncovered by economists and psychologists have caught on with the general public, influencing countless life decisions.

But it turns out that there are two popular insights that we need to unlearn—because they haven't held up to close scrutiny:

1. Have you heard that happiness caps out at an income of $75,000 a year, and earning more than that won't further boost our happiness?
2. Have you heard that 50% of life satisfaction is determined by our happiness set point and 10% by our life's circumstances—which means the remaining 40% is up to us?

Both ideas are appealing. We like the idea that those with far higher incomes aren't necessarily happier. We like the idea that we have plenty of room to improve our own happiness. That likely explains why these two notions have become so popular. But two studies suggest neither may be true.

Capping out

Happiness research traces its origins to a 1974 study by economist Richard Easterlin. He found that, while the standard of living in the U.S. and elsewhere had climbed over time, reported happiness hadn't. It seems we care less about our absolute income and more about how we compare to others. This trend has continued, with happiness levels barely budging in the U.S. over the past half-century, despite our rising standard of living.

Does that mean that those with lower incomes are destined, on average, to be less happy? A 2010 study offered hope. It found that, while folks with higher incomes were more likely to express satisfaction with their life, earning a huge income didn't necessarily result in greater day-to-day happiness. In fact, the study found that, on average, day-to-day happiness capped out at around $75,000 in annual income and didn't improve if you earned more.

But newer research debunks this finding, and convincingly so.[1] This study involved more than 33,000 working-age Americans, who—using an app—were queried regularly throughout the day about their feelings, offering a real-time look at their emotional state. It turns out that happiness doesn't cap out at $75,000, but instead keeps climbing.

To be sure, the new study didn't find that happiness rose in lockstep with income. Instead, the gap in reported well-being between folks earning $20,000 and those earning $60,000 was similar to the difference between a $60,000 household and one that earns $180,000. The implication: As income rises, it takes more and more money to make a noticeable difference in well-being. Still, more dollars did help.

Does this mean money definitely buys happiness? Conceivably, the causation could run the other way: Maybe happier people tend to earn more. The results could also partly reflect a "focusing illusion": Higher-income participants in the study, knowing they're relatively fortunate, might have been more inclined to give positive responses when asked about their emotional state.

Even if the results hold up to further scrutiny, and I suspect they will, we're talking here about averages. The ornery old guy down the road may indeed be rich and miserable. Moreover, while money may bolster happiness, it's hardly the only ingredient in a happy life. Other

---

1 Matthew A. Killingsworth, "Experienced well-being rises with income, even above $75,000 per year," *Psychological and Cognitive Sciences*, Vol. 118, No. 4.

factors—notably the state of our health, the robustness of our social network and how we choose to spend our time—are also crucial.

Boosting happiness

A 2005 study offered a compelling way to think about happiness, all captured in a simple pie chart labeled, "What Determines Happiness?" The chart had three slices: set point at 50%, circumstances at 10% and intentional activity at 40%.

In other words, 60% of our individual happiness might be the result of a genetically determined set point and difficult-to-change life circumstances—things like where we live, what job we have and how much we make. But, the study contended, the other 40% depends on how we choose to lead our life.

Not surprisingly, this notion was eagerly embraced, especially by the self-help movement. Happiness, it seemed, was within our control. But is it? A 2019 study argues there may be less room for improvement than the earlier research suggested.[2]

The study's authors write that, "The idea that individuals' life circumstances account for only 10% of the variance in well-being seems to be based on a misunderstanding... Likewise, there is only very limited evidence to place the figure for the heritability of well-being as low as (precisely) 50%. Consequently, there is little reason to believe that 40% is a reliable estimate of the variance in chronic happiness attributable to intentional activity."

The bottom line: We don't have as much control over our happiness as we'd like to think. But that doesn't mean we can't boost our happiness a little by, say, volunteering, making more time for friends and family, avoiding unnecessary financial stress and favoring experiences over possessions. Such steps may be life enhancing, but we shouldn't kid ourselves: They probably aren't life altering.

---

2   Nicholas J. L. Brown and Julia M. Rohrer, "Easy as (Happiness) Pie? A Critical Evaluation of a Popular Model of the Determinants of Well-Being," *Journal of Happiness Studies*, Vol. 21.

Choosing Happiness

We all want to lead happier lives, but that's no easy task. Our first stumbling block: Most of us aren't even sure how to define happiness.

Fortunately, philosophers and psychologists have come to the rescue, suggesting that there are two different types of happiness. First up: hedonic happiness. Think of a wonderful party with delicious food, sparkling conversation and all your favorite people in attendance. There's great momentary pleasure and—fingers crossed—scant pain involved.

Meanwhile, eudaimonic happiness comes from leading a life filled with meaning and purpose. Forget the amusement park, the martini or the shopping spree. Instead, think about things like volunteering, writing a novel, training for a marathon or launching your own business. We're talking about activities that we think are important, we're passionate about, we find challenging and we feel we're good at. These sorts of meaningful, fulfilling activities might allow us to enjoy a Mihaly Csikszentmihalyi moment of "flow" and get us to the top of Abraham Maslow's hierarchy of needs, where we achieve "self-actualization."

It seems any boost in hedonic happiness tends to be fleeting, and we soon return to our personal set point—our base level of happiness. This is the idea behind the so-called hedonic treadmill, where we constantly strive for greater happiness, only to find ourselves running in place. Meanwhile, increases in eudaimonic happiness have the potential to be longer lasting, but such increases also take far more effort.

This division between hedonic and eudaimonic happiness, which has been debated as far back as the fourth century BC, has moral overtones. How so? Hedonic happiness seems like the easy choice. You go out in the evening for a few drinks with friends and feel temporarily happier, but in the morning you're back to your base level of happiness and—who knows—perhaps even feeling a little hungover. By contrast, eudaimonic happiness can appeal to our puritanical streak. There's work involved and challenges to overcome, so it feels more virtuous. We're striving to be better versions of ourselves and, while we're at it, perhaps also improving the world around us.

Are the two types of happiness mutually exclusive? Yes and no. Imagine making a sumptuous dinner and then sharing it with friends. There would be the eudaimonic happiness associated with preparing a great meal and then the hedonic pleasure of enjoying it with others. You get both types of happiness—but you get them at different times.

Since the 1970s, happiness research has delivered a host of useful insights. There's the well-known notion that we tend to get greater happiness from experiences rather than possessions. There's the idea that happiness through life is U-shaped, with our reported level of happiness falling through our first few decades as adults, bottoming out in our 40s and then rebounding from there. There's the idea that what matters to our happiness isn't our absolute standard of living, but how we stand relative to those around us—which is why we don't want to be the family with a six-figure salary in a neighborhood full of seven-figure income earners.

To this array of insights, I think the distinction between hedonic and eudaimonic happiness is a great addition, one that could help us lead a better life. And, no, I don't think we should favor one to the exclusion of the other. Instead, we should try to design a life for ourselves where we enjoy both.

We're all constrained by money and time. As we think about how to allocate those two limited resources, it's worth pondering the cost associated with each type of happiness. It strikes me that hedonic happiness usually comes with a higher price tag, while eudaimonic happiness involves a greater investment of time. If we go to a lavish restaurant, we'll get hedonic happiness—and a big bill at the end. But if we decide to learn the piano, we may enjoy long-lasting eudaimonic happiness, but the cost will be a hefty commitment of time.

For those in the workforce, the inclination will be to favor hedonic happiness because, in the course of a busy workweek and perhaps with children to raise, time is in short supply. What about eudaimonic happiness? It is, of course, worth striving for, but it'll take discipline and good time management. Indeed, for those in the workforce, perhaps the best hope for eudaimonic happiness is to find a job they love.

Retirees, by contrast, may have fewer years ahead of them, but more free time during the course of any given week. If we've done a good job of saving, we should have the money needed to buy hedonic happiness. But hedonic happiness alone won't make for a fulfilling retirement. That's where that free time comes in. How will we convert those hours into eudaimonic happiness? For those of us in or near retirement, it's a crucially important question.

8.
Cancer

I N THE WEEKS after my diagnosis, the doctors had me on a high dose of steroids that regularly had me awake at 2:30 a.m., wired and ready to go. Aware that time was short, I poured my early morning energy into my laptop, writing one article after another, as I pondered the financial and other implications of my terminal cancer.

Perhaps no set of articles I've ever written has received such rapt attention. My articles and my diagnosis even caught the attention of the national press. *The New York Times* wrote about my illness, and *The Washington Post*, *The Wall Street Journal*, *AARP The Magazine* and *The Telegraph* of London all asked me to pen articles. Early in my career, I'd been renowned as a relentless advocate of indexing. Now, it seemed, I was gaining notoriety once again—for dying.

Death is a fairly frequent topic for articles, but the participants usually aren't the authors. Most can't write about their own demise, either because death comes suddenly or because they slip away amid cognitive decline. Still, I was surprised by the response to my pieces. I was repeatedly told I was brave to write about my diagnosis. It didn't seem brave to me. Over the decades, I'd written about so many aspects of my own life. Why wouldn't I write about my illness?

The reaction to my cancer articles tells me that death is still taboo and that those who are ailing are expected to quietly exit the stage. One result: Death is more frightening than it should be. I know my demise is coming and I know some pain will be involved. But I've had a wonderfully full life and managed to achieve a reasonable amount. Sure, I'd love to have the time to do more. But at this late hour, perhaps I'm finally ready to declare "enough."

Maybe.

The C Word

On Sunday morning, May 19, 2024, I was enjoying croissants and coffee with Elaine at the kitchen table, while watching the neighborhood sparrows, finches, cardinals and squirrels have their way with the bird feeder. All was right in our little world, except I was a little wobbly when walking—the result, I suspected, of balance issues caused by an ear infection.

It was going to be a busy week, and I figured that it would be smart to get some antibiotics inside me, even if visiting the urgent care clinic on Sunday might be more expensive than contacting my primary care physician on Monday and perhaps having to go in for an appointment.

Long story short, I ended the day in the intensive care unit of a local hospital, where the staff discovered lung cancer that had metastasized to my brain and a few other spots. My prognosis was not good. I quickly received three brain radiation treatments and started chemotherapy, but these steps were merely deferring death and perhaps not for very long. I'll spare you the gory medical details. But as best I could gather from my oncologist at that time, I had just a dozen okay months ahead of me.

Weirdly, at that juncture, I felt pretty darn good, and perhaps better than most 61-year-olds. Every morning, I was stretching and lifting for 20 minutes, and then riding a stationary bike for 40 minutes. And in case you're curious, I was never much of a smoker and last had a cigarette in 1987, when I was age 24. Instead, it seems my lung cancer was the result of a defective gene—one that's rare and without a promising treatment plan.

Here were my initial financial thoughts on receiving my diagnosis.

Managing money is fraught with uncertainty, but never more so than now

There's much I don't know—how long I'll live, how long I'll be able to do the work I love, what my medical and other costs will be. Still, on this score, I'm hardly alone. In varying degrees, we all face this sort of uncertainty, and it's one reason managing money is so fascinating.

Money is intimately bound up with regret

We often berate ourselves for the foolish purchases and investments we make. This one has been a pleasant surprise: Until the past few years, I've lived quite frugally, and yet I find myself with almost no regrets about that lifestyle. Yes, if my health allows, I'll be ticking off some bucket-list items. But mostly what I feel is profound gratitude for the life I've had. I've had amazing opportunities and wonderful experiences, and that allows me to face the time ahead with surprising equanimity.

The cliché is true: Something like this makes you truly appreciate life

Despite those bucket-list items, I find my greatest joy comes from small, inexpensive daily pleasures: that first cup of coffee, exercise, friends and family, a good meal, writing and editing, smiles from strangers, the sunshine on my face. If we can keep life's less admirable emotions at bay, the world is a wonderful place.

We can control risk, but we can't eliminate it

I've spent decades managing both financial risk and potential threats to my health. But despite such precautions, sometimes we get blindsided.

There have been few cancer occurrences in my family, and it's never been something I had reason to fear. Chance is a cruel mistress.

It's toughest on those left behind

I'll be gone, but Elaine and my family will remain, and they'll have to navigate the world without me. I so want them to be okay, financially and emotionally, and that's driving many of the steps I'm now taking.

Generosity suddenly feels so much sweeter

No doubt part of the reason is that I'll no longer need most of my retirement savings, plus there's scant reason to acquire new possessions. Perhaps part of me is also more anxious to earn the good opinion of others, while I still have the chance.

But there's another aspect to this: As I watch friends and family react to my diagnosis, it makes me appreciate that most folks have an inherent goodness and they're constantly struggling to do the right thing, and a little generosity is a way to acknowledge that.

Life's priorities become crystal clear

Even at this late stage, I believe it's important to have a sense of purpose, both professionally and personally. I can't do much about the fewer years, and I have no anger about their loss. But I do want the time ahead to be happy, productive and meaningful.

I've been moving to further simplify my finances, organize my affairs and make things right with those around me. Underlying this is a desire to control what I can—hardly surprising, given the uncertainty swirling around me. Still, I'm probably overdoing it.

Looking Different

I've always assumed my financial life wasn't so different from that of others—and that made writing personal finance articles a whole lot easier. I, too, wanted to own a home, buy the right insurance, pay for the kids' college, and amass enough for a long and comfortable retirement.

On top of that, I wasn't some financial minority—a highly paid executive, or a successful business owner, or the recipient of a hefty inheritance. Instead, I was like most everybody else, trying to turn an everyday paycheck into something that looked like financial success.

But suddenly, I am the oddball. I'm in my early 60s with perhaps less than a year to live, and that means my financial life today doesn't look like that of anybody I know—in seven key ways.

1. I no longer need to worry about funding retirement

That money I diligently amassed over the past four decades? Almost all of it will end up with my heirs. My carefully considered plans—continuing to work at least part time, buying a series of immediate-fixed annuities that generate lifetime income, delaying Social Security until age 70—have gone out the window.

Of course, I had no clue my life would take this turn, so it makes no sense to regret the thought and money that I poured into retirement planning. Still, it's sobering to think that I devoted a big chunk of my life to an endeavor that'll do me scant good.

2. It doesn't matter how much I spend—in theory

Should I start splurging? Even before my cancer diagnosis, Elaine and I had two trips to Europe planned for 2024. We nixed one and revamped the other, so the timing fitted with my chemotherapy schedule.

When I made changes to our flights, the airlines dinged me for a few hundred dollars. Supposedly, I no longer need to worry about how much I spend, and yet I couldn't help but be irked. Yes, even now, my frugality still lingers.

In addition to the European trip we kept, we booked three new trips for 2024. None was cheap. But again, even at this late stage, there's a limit to how wide I'll open my wallet. I looked at the price of business class flights and, for some trips, I just couldn't bring myself to do it.

My plan was to add even more trips. I enjoy the planning and I like having things on the calendar to look forward to. But caution suggests I should wait until I have a better handle on how fast my health is deteriorating.

3. My portfolio's time horizon just got longer

I'm not a long-term investor anymore, but Elaine and my two kids are, and at this point they're the ones I'm investing for. The upshot: I have more than 90% of my portfolio in stocks—because that's the asset allocation that makes sense for them, given where they are in their careers and what other investments they hold.

Two days after my diagnosis, I sat down with Elaine and the kids, and talked to them about my estate. One thing I emphasized to my two 30-something children: They'll be getting their inheritance far earlier than expected—but, if they're smart in handling the money, they'll end up as wealthy retirees. With some three decades to retirement, the money that Hannah and Henry inherit could grow eightfold.

How did I get to eightfold? According to the rule of 72, if money grows at an after-inflation rate of 7% a year, its real value would double after ten years, quadruple after 20 years and be up eightfold after 30 years. To be honest, I'm not sure the stock market will fare that well. Still, using 7% made the math easy, and I'm hoping the potential growth impressed Hannah and Henry.

4. Estate planning has become my top priority

My financial focus today is on giving away money and getting my affairs in order. In recent years, I've been moving to simplify my finances. Yet my diagnosis has made me realize there's still much to be done.

Indeed, if my life had come to an abrupt end, I now realize my family would have had a surprising amount of work to do to settle my affairs. Fortunately, I can now do a lot of that work for them. Make no mistake: Leaving behind a well-organized financial life is a wonderful gift to your family.

5. I can stop fretting over my retirement's tax bill

In recent years, I've been focused on the hefty income tax bills I'd face once I reached age 75 and had to start taking required minimum distributions (RMDs) from my retirement accounts. I'd also worried about the Medicare premium surcharges known as IRMAA, or income-related monthly adjustment amount, that would kick in at age 65. But thanks to my cancer diagnosis, living that long is highly unlikely.

With an eye to minimizing both RMDs and IRMAA later in retirement, I'd shrunk my traditional IRA by making large Roth conversions. A lot of number-crunching lay behind those conversions. But like my lifetime focus on retirement, all that thought devoted to future taxes now looks like a heap of wasted time. That said, there is a silver lining: Those conversions will mean a handsome inheritance for my two kids, who are my Roth's beneficiaries.

6. Many worries of other 60-somethings are no longer my concern

I won't need to choose between traditional Medicare and Medicare Advantage. I can forget about long-term-care costs. I don't need to fret over how long I'll be able to stay in my home or whether I ought to move into some form of senior housing.

These are all topics others in their 60s should be thinking about, and I've certainly given them a lot of thought in recent years. Even now, my web browser's bookmarks include those for local continuing care retirement communities (CCRCs) that Elaine and I thought we'd visit down the road. But while Elaine will need to ponder the possibility of a CCRC, senior housing disappeared from my list of concerns the moment I got my diagnosis.

7. Social Security has become a different sort of conundrum

I could have claimed Social Security in January 2025, when I turned age 62. But I didn't.

Instead, my focus is on the best strategy not for me, but for Elaine. How can she get the most out of Social Security? She could claim either her own benefit or she could claim survivor benefits based on my earnings record, with the option of later swapping from one benefit to the other. It's an intriguing situation—one I'm currently researching.

No Slowing Down

Who has time to die? I never realized death would be so busy.

I thought I had my financial affairs in good order. But in the two months following my cancer diagnosis, I made countless financial tweaks, mostly with a view to making things easier after my death for my wife Elaine and my two children.

Here are just some of the steps I've taken:

- I took my two checking accounts—my personal account and the business account for HumbleDollar—and made Elaine the joint account holder with rights of survivorship. One reason for the switch: My personal account is automatically debited for all utilities and other household bills, and the change in titling should make it easier for Elaine to keep tabs on things after my death.
- I've cancelled two of my four credit cards, and plan to cancel one more once I've used the rewards I've accumulated. That'll leave just one card. Elaine has two cards of her own, so we'll have a backup if a card gets hacked, lost or stolen during the trips we have planned for the months ahead.
- I closed a small IRA I inherited from my father in 2009. It had just $6,700 in it, but I'd hung on to it, partly for sentimental reasons and partly to avoid the income tax bill triggered by liquidating the account. But after my diagnosis, I figured shutting down the account would be one less thing for my family to deal with.
- I rolled over the solo 401(k) I had at Vanguard Group—which was all Roth dollars—into my Roth IRA. That, too, means one less

thing to deal with after my death. Even before my diagnosis, I was irked that Vanguard was turning over administration of its solo 401(k) operation to another company, another tell-tale sign of the firm's weak commitment to less important lines of business. But with my diagnosis, I also realized I was less interested in saving for the future and more focused on giving, and that's where my extra dollars will go from now on, rather than into my solo 401(k).

- I'm in the middle of getting a new will, along with medical and financial powers of attorney. Yes, I'm finally getting those powers of attorney—a missing piece of my financial life that I'd acknowledged last year and which triggered some well-deserved tut-tutting from commenters.

- I tweaked my IRA's beneficiary designations. My two children will split my Roth IRA, which seems like the tax-smart way to go, because emptying that account over ten years won't mean extra taxable income on top of their current salaries. Meanwhile, Elaine and my kids will share my traditional IRA, with its embedded income-tax bill.

- I added Elaine as the beneficiary of my modest health savings account and the variable annuity I bought through Vanguard more than two decades ago. I purchased the latter when I was maxing out on my other retirement accounts and looking for further tax-deferred growth. Like its solo 401(k) operation, Vanguard's variable annuity business was unceremoniously turned over to another financial firm, in this case Transamerica.

- I have a few banker's boxes of financial papers stashed in the basement, which I'm now in the midst of pruning. Among other things, those boxes include every tax return since 1986, when I moved to the New York area from London. Yes, there's some serious shredding to be done.

- I forgave the private mortgage I wrote for my daughter in 2015. That'll necessitate me filing a gift-tax return for 2024, thereby reducing my $13.61 million federal estate-tax exemption. But given that my estate won't be worth anywhere close to $13.61 million, there's no financial downside.

- I've also made financial gifts to my new grandson and son. If I don't live for 12 months after making these various gifts, all concerned—my so-called lineal descendants—will face Pennsylvania's 4.5% inheritance tax on all but $3,000 of the gifts. That isn't an issue with Elaine, who as my spouse isn't subject to the inheritance tax. Even before my diagnosis, we'd planned to get married. We moved up the date when I got the bad news.

There's still more to come: I need to move various insurance policies—such as homeowner's, flood and umbrella liability—into Elaine's name. Ditto for various utility bills. I also need to make Elaine the person responsible for purchasing the various technology services that keep HumbleDollar humming along. And we're still trying to figure out the best Social Security claiming strategy for Elaine, knowing she may be able to receive my benefit as a survivor benefit.

On the Clock

First was the voice of my father's friend. Then a policeman came on the line. While riding his bicycle, my 75-year-old father had been struck and killed by a speeding driver.

That was 2009. There were no goodbyes. Instead, seared into my memory are the photograph I was shown at the hospital, so I could identify my father's body, and the details in his final medical report, which I never should have read.

My death will be far different. I've been given the time to straighten out my financial affairs, savor some last experiences, spend time with friends and family, and set HumbleDollar on a course that I hope will ensure it continues to thrive.

Needless to say, my version of death seems preferable. Like everybody else, I have a finite lifespan, but mine involves far less uncertainty. My truncated time has brought into sharp focus what's important and what isn't. I refuse to spend my remaining time being angry about my cancer diagnosis, or feeling cheated, or wondering why I got the defective cancer-causing gene, or bouncing from one cancer center to another in search of a cure that doesn't exist.

Instead, I'm determined to make the most of every day, doing what I love and trying mightily to fend off life's nonsense. It's an attitude I recommend—one I'd encourage you to embrace now, rather than waiting for a dire medical prognosis. We should never forget that our most precious resource isn't money, but time.

I'm no fan of motivational speeches and feel-good pop psychology. Still, at this moment, I'm willing to embrace one piece of bumper-sticker wisdom: Happiness is a choice. It's highly likely that my days will draw to a close within the next few years—for those with my diagnosis, the median life expectancy is 16 months—and there isn't a whole lot I can do about it, other than follow the treatment plan, eat healthily and continue to exercise. But I can strive to make the most of the days I'm granted.

So, what do I mean by "choosing happiness"? No, I'm not angling to have some laughs and a few drinks with buddies. Rather, I have a vision of the future that I want to see fulfilled. I want to die knowing I've built something—a sound future for my two kids, a good life for Elaine, and a solid path forward for HumbleDollar. If I can put the necessary pieces in place, I'll be happy.

Crazy as it sounds, Elaine and I are even planning to remodel the upstairs bathroom, with all the disruption that'll be involved. It's something we discussed before my diagnosis. I want to get the work done for Elaine's sake, plus the feeling of accomplishment would make me happy. Yes, despite the late hour, making progress still gives me a profound sense of satisfaction.

Even as I strive to make the most of the here and now, sadness occasionally creeps in. I find myself pondering the retirement years I won't have with Elaine, or how my three-year-old grandson will have scant memory of me, or how I'll be nothing but a photograph to his newborn younger brother. Such moments sometimes hit me in the early morning, when I'm alone in the basement, spinning away on the stationary bicycle, the tears mixing with the sweat.

Moments of irritation also occasionally creep in. Soon after I got my diagnosis, it seemed the insurance company was dragging its feet, taking far too long to approve my treatment plan. I was bothered by the delay. But mostly, I was bothered that this bothered me—that I was wasting time being angry at some lumbering, unresponsive insurance company. That meant a day that wasn't as good as it could be.

Still, despite the brief moments of sadness and irritation, the days seem pretty good right now. I'm continuing to work hard to keep HumbleDollar chugging along and to prep the site for a future without me. I'm spending more time with Elaine and my kids. I'm feeling mostly fine and, indeed, my only major complaints are the disrupted sleep that accompanies the steroids I'm taking and the fatigue caused by the chemotherapy.

I'm hoping this happy state will last for at least another year, but there are no guarantees. What about when the end comes? It's hard to know what it'll be like—which part of my body will give way, how much discomfort and pain will be involved, and how clear my thinking will be at that juncture. Still, in my wishful thinking, I have a mental picture of how it'll play out.

After decades of pushing myself far too hard, I like to think I'll gracefully acknowledge that cancer has the upper hand. And that's when I'll cut myself some slack, I'll give in to the morphine offered by the hospice nurse and I'll drift off, finally getting the sleep my body hungers for. Reality, of course, will be far messier. But this is the story I tell to comfort myself.

A Time to Give

Death and taxes are inevitable—and, as I keep getting reminded, also inextricably entwined.

I'm not so fortunate that I need worry about federal estate taxes. That privilege belongs to those who die with $13.61 million in 2024. But that doesn't mean the taxman isn't hovering over my demise, raising a host of lesser issues.

Paying the piper

Over the past few years, my focus has been on making big Roth conversions while staying within the 24% federal income-tax bracket. The goal: Build up my Roth and then bequeath it to my two children, while also shrinking my traditional IRA, so required minimum distributions in my 70s and beyond wouldn't push me into a much higher income-tax bracket.

For 2024, I'm still aiming for the top of the 24% tax bracket—but I'm not planning any more Roth conversions. Instead, given my cancer diagnosis and likely short life expectancy, my new focus is on making gifts to my wife Elaine, my two children and my two grandchildren. Federal estate taxes may not be a worry, but Pennsylvania's inheritance tax is. The latter isn't an issue for Elaine, because spouses are exempt. But it'll nick 4.5% out of any money I bequeath to my kids and grandkids.

The inheritance tax could also take a bite out of the money I give them now if I don't live at least a year after making those gifts. That creates an incentive to give away money as soon as possible, and I've been doing just that. How much could I give? In the past, I've been guided by the gift-tax exclusion, which is $18,000 in 2024.

That's the amount anybody can give another person each year without filing a gift-tax return. Anything above that sum gets deducted from the sum you can bequeath free of federal estate taxes, and would necessitate filing a gift-tax return. But given that I won't be bequeathing anything close to the $13.61 million federal estate-tax exclusion, gifting more than $18,000 is no big deal.

The money I'm giving away is coming from a mix of my earned income and withdrawals from my traditional IRA. I have roughly 10% of my overall IRA—both Roth and traditional—in bonds, and I'm dipping into those bonds to make gifts. I may also sell some bonds to cover living costs if my earned income is less than I expect or if our travel expenses prove greater than I imagine. In my mental accounting, I'm free to use this bond-market money during my lifetime.

Passing it on

The other 90% of my overall IRA—again both Roth and traditional— is earmarked for Elaine and the kids, and that money is entirely in stocks. While my time horizon is now short, that of my beneficiaries hasn't changed. Fingers crossed, they should have plenty of time to ride out any stock market downturn and notch handsome gains.

Elaine will be able to treat my IRA as her own and draw it down over her lifetime. Meanwhile, my two kids will be required to empty the IRA money they inherit over ten years. Hannah and Henry will also owe Pennsylvania's inheritance tax on the money.

All the money for Elaine is coming from my traditional IRA, while my two children will get my Roth accounts, plus a portion of my traditional IRA. Why earmark the entire Roth for Hannah and Henry? All their withdrawals will be tax-free. That means those withdrawals, when layered on top of their earned income, won't push them into a higher tax bracket.

I briefly pondered withdrawing from my Roth and giving the money to the kids now. If I live a year after making those gifts, they'd avoid the Pennsylvania's inheritance tax. But the fact is, even a modest amount of tax-free growth would pay for the inheritance tax, so it's better to leave the Roth untouched and let the kids empty the account.

The IRS recently issued rules compelling some IRA beneficiaries to empty the accounts gradually over ten years, but those rules won't affect my kids. I've told Hannah and Henry they should delay tapping the Roth until near the end of the ten-year withdrawal period, so they squeeze the most out of the tax-free growth. Meanwhile, my kids should probably draw down the traditional IRA slowly over the ten years, so they spread out the taxable income, plus they can use their withdrawal in the year after my death to pay Pennsylvania's inheritance tax.

Do I now regret my earlier Roth conversions, and the big tax bills I paid as a result? Far from it. My best guess is that the tax arbitrage has worked in my family's favor, meaning the tax rate I paid on my Roth conversions is less than what my children would now face if I hadn't made those conversions, and they were instead looking at emptying a big traditional IRA.

Taxing matters

Back in 2015, I wrote a mortgage to help my daughter purchase her current home. In July 2024, I forgave the loan. That loan forgiveness is potentially subject to the state's inheritance tax if I don't live at least a year after making that gift. Still, I'm assured the forgiven loan won't be considered taxable income for Hannah—something that could happen if, say, you're drowning in credit card debt and persuade your card company to forgive that debt.

That brings me to two other tax issues—one I'm no longer focused on, one that could be an issue. The new non-issue: the Medicare premium surcharge known as IRMAA, or income-related monthly adjustment amount. Before my cancer diagnosis, I'd planned to limit my taxable income starting in 2026, when I would turn age 63. Why? My IRMAA surcharges two years later, when I'm 65 and qualify for Medicare, would be based on that income. But now, it's unlikely I'll live that long.

Meanwhile, I've been assiduously tracking my medical expenses in 2024, thinking I'd be able to deduct them on Schedule A. But at $29,200, the standard deduction for a couple is sufficiently high in 2024 that I now suspect I won't have enough itemized deductions, especially given that my health insurance has a $5,800 out-of-pocket maximum and given that these expenses are only deductible if they exceed 7.5% of adjusted gross income. Still, that relatively low out-of-pocket maximum is a godsend. I hate to think how much I'd be paying out of pocket if my cancer treatment was happening before the 2010 passage of the Affordable Care Act.

No Regrets

My first reaction on hearing my cancer diagnosis: I'm okay with this. My reaction a few hours later: I'm being self-centered.

My time is short, though how short remains an open question. Still, my truncated life expectancy makes something of a mockery of my pre-diagnosis comments about how we should view retirement not as the finish line, but rather as the beginning of a journey that might last two or three decades and perhaps account for almost half of our adult life.

Despite that, I feel no anger, sadness or fear about what lies ahead. While I'm going to do all that I can to extend my life, until all reasonable measures are exhausted, I'm not devastated by the thought that my life will be cut short. Why not? As I look back— yes, I suddenly find myself in the "summing up" phase—I feel great gratitude for the life I've been able to lead.

The fact is, I've had wonderful opportunities and experiences, and I consider myself very fortunate. Below are nine reasons I feel grateful. One thing that struck me about my list: While money is a factor in Nos. 1, 5 and especially 6, it's of little or no importance to the other six items.

1. For most of my career, I've done work I thoroughly enjoy

Even today, I happily get up far too early, make a cup of coffee, and immediately start writing and editing. The only exception to this happy story was my six years at Citigroup, when—toward the end—I felt I was wasting my time and making scant difference in the world.

2. I've known enough bad times to have perspective

Everybody has rough periods, and it might seem like those times have no silver lining. But I'd argue bad times teach us who we are and nudge us toward a more nuanced view of the world. No, I have no desire to spend another nine years at English boarding school, or cope again with the aftermath of my father's death, or have two wives leave me. But those experiences helped make me who I am, and I like to think they've knocked off some of the rough edges and pushed me to appreciate life more.

3. I have a close-knit family

I have two children and, so far, two grandkids. I also have an 85-year-old mother and three siblings, and—all these decades later—we all remain surprisingly close. I hear about so many fractured families, where old wounds fester and folks refuse to talk to one another. Somehow, we've avoided that fate.

4. I got the chance to push myself to my physical limits

As a schoolboy, I was scornful of athletic endeavors and made scant effort. That changed in my 30s, when I became intrigued by the idea of running a marathon. I ended up running four marathons and five half-marathons, including a half-marathon around the deck of a boat floating off the coast of Antarctica. I also ran a slew of local 5k, five-mile and ten-mile road races, finishing first on a dozen occasions. My dodgy right Achilles means I can no longer run, but I can still recall the pleasure of emptying myself during the final miles of a race.

5. I've had the opportunity to see much of the world

Not long before I turned age ten, my father was posted to Bangladesh for four years, giving us the chance to see much of the region. I've traveled often to Europe, and my children's studies have meant I've spent time in Senegal, Egypt and Turkey. Sure, there are places I'd still like to see—and, at this point, probably won't—but I don't feel shortchanged.

6. While I worried a lot about money in my 20s and 30s, I haven't worried much since

As I've come to appreciate, that's rare: For far too many folks, money casts a dark shadow over every day, and escaping those worries can seem like an impossible task.

7. On a handful of occasions, I've felt like I had the world's attention

A few times, I've appeared on major television shows, triggering phone calls and emails from folks I hadn't heard from in years. When I was at *The Wall Street Journal*, I wrote some articles that prompted 500-plus complimentary emails. Such moments were rare enough to seem special—and sufficiently infrequent that my ego didn't remain inflated for long.

8. I'm getting to spend my final days with someone I love deeply and who loves me

In the middle of the night, when dark thoughts derail my sleep, it's wonderful to rest my hand on Elaine's arm and draw comfort from her stillness.

9. I've been afforded the time to contemplate my own death

There will be no sudden demise or slow slide into dementia. How would you change your life if you knew you had just a year or two to live? I'm getting the chance to answer that question, and I consider it a great privilege.

Still, all of this is a tad selfish. I may not be racked with regret and sadness over my early departure from this life—but arguably I'm the lucky one. As I've come to realize, it isn't me who is suffering, but rather those who will be left behind, and especially Elaine, who will need to build a life without me.

I have the chance to make my peace with my fate, while Elaine and other family members must grapple with all the uncertainty that'll follow. I'm trying to make the most of each day I have left, even as they're grieving—and my refusal to join in their grieving creates a void that makes it more difficult for them.

Four Questions

I'm writing this piece seven months since I received my terminal diagnosis. Cancer is now the reality that looms over each day, and it's been a rocky road, though the latest abdomen scan suggests I'll be around for a while longer.

Where's my head at? Here are four questions I've been asking myself—questions, I suspect, that might also be interesting to those who aren't facing a terminal diagnosis.

1. Am I afraid of dying?

No, but I am afraid of not living. In particular, there are two things I'll miss.

First, I love the day to day—the blue sky, leaves dancing down the sidewalk, morning coffee, afternoon naps, an evening glass of wine, chatting about the day with Elaine. Words like mindful and intentional tend to hit my gag reflex—too touchy-feely for my taste. Still, I'm trying to be mindful of all that's around me and intentional about how I use my time. The world is an amazing place, and I hate the idea that I'll no longer get to revel in its daily joys.

Second, it pains me that not only won't I get to grow old with Elaine, but also I won't see what the years ahead hold for my children and grandchildren. Who will they become? What triumphs will they enjoy? How will they cope with the hardships thrown their way? Most of us get to the point where we focus less on our own life, and instead live more through the eyes of others. I was just starting to enjoy that new life phase, but now it's about to get snatched away.

2. Am I using my time in the best way possible?

Mostly, I've spent the past seven months doing what I've done for years, which is to sit at my laptop, writing and editing. Maybe this work doesn't bring happiness in a laugh-out-loud kind of way, but it does give me a profound sense of satisfaction.

Are there other things I ought to be doing? Even before my diagnosis, Elaine and I had a travel wish list. Over the past seven months, we've managed three trips. But we've also canceled one because I landed in hospital—and we're aware that, from now on, every plan we make is tentative. It feels like time is increasingly short, the world is getting smaller, venturing far from our Philadelphia home is more daunting, and perhaps our "bucket list" time could soon be over.

Am I upset? When you know time is running low, it makes you think hard about how you use your days and weeks. Would I be distraught if I never went to Europe again? Probably not. Instead, what I fear most is the moment when I no longer have the energy to make some small difference in the world, which is why you'll find me sitting in front of my laptop tomorrow, and the day after, and—I hope—the day after that.

3. Why aren't I angrier about my diagnosis?

I consider myself fortunate. I've spent my career doing what I love and—despite some rough times—I've had a mostly happy life. What if it had been otherwise? If I'd been stuck in a job I hated, waiting for retirement to get my reward, I imagine I would indeed feel cheated, and I wouldn't be nearly so sanguine about my diagnosis.

Do you hate your job? Are you in an unhappy relationship? Suppose that, like me, you were given a year to live. Would you regret the life you've led and, if so, should you take steps to change it now?

4. How can I prepare to be my future self?

Previously, I wrote, "As best I can tell, my stage 4 cancer hasn't had any impact on my physical abilities. Indeed, most days, I feel pretty good. I'd always thought death would be easier to accept because of the pain involved and the endless interactions with the medical establishment, which would slowly sap my will to live. But so far, it hasn't been that way."

Ironically, it was about then that I started feeling a whole lot worse, thanks to the back pain caused by the cancer spreading to my spine. Radiation earlier this month brought substantial relief. Nonetheless, I feel my illness has moved me fast forward into old age. It can be difficult to imagine who we'll become—but, as I've discovered, there's a risk we'll become that person with extraordinary speed. How can we better prepare ourselves? In retrospect, I'm grateful for two lifelong habits.

First, before my diagnosis, I was in good physical shape, and that's stood me in good stead over the past seven months. I've worked out pretty much every day for three decades, ever since I started training for my first marathon. Clearly, this didn't stop one of my genes from going rogue and causing cancer. On the other hand, because I was in good shape when I got my diagnosis, it's helped me to weather the treatment reasonably well and, I believe, bought me a little extra time.

Second, my financial affairs were fairly well organized before my diagnosis. Since then, I've made a big push to simplify my finances even further, and to throw out old papers and unwanted possessions. The amount of work has been significant. Still, without my earlier efforts, it would have been far more onerous.

9.
Money Meets Life

I FIGURED THAT, AFTER early 2025, there was a decent chance I wouldn't have the energy to do a lot of writing and editing. What should my final articles for HumbleDollar be about? I quickly settled on the theme that has increasingly preoccupied me—the intersection between money and who we are, what we want and what we think we want.

The result was the six articles that follow, which were part of a series I dubbed "money meets life." They weren't the best articles I've written. But they were a far cry from what I first wrote about in the late 1980s, when my focus was on mutual fund expenses, turnover ratios, five-year performance comparisons, stock-picking styles and other mechanics of investing.

Yes, it's important to grasp the investment basics. But it's much more important to have a good handle on what we want from money, what frightens and emboldens us, and who or what influences our financial choices. We all like to think we act rationally. But it just isn't so, and that means it takes a heap of self-awareness to make smart money decisions.

Money Grows Up

I moved from London to New York City in 1986, when I was age 23. That's when my financial education truly began.

I'd previously studied economics for three years and spent a year writing about the international financial markets for *Euromoney* magazine. Still, I knew almost nothing about investing, insurance, homeownership and other topics crucial to managing a household's finances.

I've learned a ton since, and the focus of that education kept changing, providing endless fodder for articles during my long career as a financial writer. The fact is, the way we think about money today is totally different from four decades ago, and that's a huge plus. How so? We're now focused less on determining the "optimal" financial products and strategies—and more on how money can be used to improve the lives of everyday individuals.

Investing

As with almost everybody else, investing was where my financial journey began. I worked at *Forbes* magazine from late 1986 to early 1990, focusing principally on mutual funds.

The standard article was the fund manager profile. It was fairly formulaic: Interview a guy (yes, it was almost always a man) with a decent track record, cook up some theme for the article, describe his investment strategy, and then offer three or four stock picks that illustrated his approach.

I felt like I wouldn't be a real journalist until I worked for a daily newspaper. That opportunity came in January 1990, when *The Wall Street Journal* hired me to write about mutual funds. But by then, it was starting to dawn on me that few star fund managers remained stars, and it was impossible to figure out ahead of time who they'd be. Thus began my passion for index funds.

As I relentlessly advocated for broadly diversified, low-cost index funds, I briefly imagined that I knew pretty much everything I needed to know about managing money. But in truth, I'd barely scratched the surface.

Personal finance

With the investing problem "solved" with index funds, I went looking for other subjects to tackle in my weekly *Journal* column, which first appeared in 1994. In the years that followed, I found myself writing about personal-finance topics such as taxes, Social Security, college funding, insurance and estate planning.

Unlike investing, where folks were unlikely to do better than a simple portfolio of low-cost index funds, there was ample room for improvement in these other areas of money management. Indeed, a modest effort could greatly bolster a family's financial position, and yet these topics were largely ignored by financial advisors and Wall Street investment houses.

Behavior

Even as I dabbled in subjects other than investing, I developed an interest in behavioral finance and evolutionary psychology. Why did investors resist indexing, despite its obvious advantages? Why did they misjudge their appetite for risk? Why do folks spend so much today and save too little for retirement?

The broad parameters of what constitutes smart financial behavior are pretty much agreed upon, even if experts might quibble about the details. Problem is, knowing the right course of action isn't enough. It's like losing weight or improving our fitness. The big issue isn't figuring out what to do. Rather, it's getting ourselves to do what we know is right. That can require a huge effort—because we need to overcome our hard-wired instincts.

Meaning

Money isn't simply the vehicle that allows us to put a roof over our head and food on the table. Instead, our relationship with money is far more complicated. We use it to try to make ourselves happier, to recreate our most treasured memories from childhood, and to tell the world who we are and what we value. In other words, we take money and we infuse it with meaning.

Around 2005 or so, I became fascinated by happiness research, and whether money can indeed boost our satisfaction with our lot in life. The answer is "yes," but the research also highlighted money's limitations. For instance, the boost to happiness from a new car or a pay raise can be remarkably brief, while the impact on happiness of a seven-figure portfolio pales in significance compared to folks' predisposition to be happy—whether they have a high or low happiness set point.

Self-knowledge

Behavioral finance helps us understand why we behave the way we do, while happiness research offers ideas for how to get more satisfaction out of our dollars. But which insights resonate the most? The answer will be different for each of us.

That brings me to what, I suspect, will be an increasing focus of the financial world: offering folks insights into who they are, so they can be better managers of their own money. How can we figure out what our true risk tolerance is? What mix of the five personality types—agreeableness, conscientiousness, extraversion, neuroticism and openness—do we possess, and how does that affect our financial decision-making? What from our past continues to play a role in the financial choices we make today? These, I think, are fascinating questions, and I suspect folks will be much better able to answer them in the years ahead.

Taking Center Stage

It's the one asset we're all born with, and it pretty much defines our financial life. I'm talking here about our human capital, our ability to pull in a paycheck.

That paycheck—or the lack thereof—drives our ability to save, service debt and take investment risk. It also dictates our insurance needs and how much emergency money we should hold. Put it all together, and our human capital should arguably determine how we manage our money over our lifetime.

Let's start with our early adult years, which are often marked by substantial borrowing as we pay for college, buy that first car and purchase a starter home. Yes, the amount of debt involved can be frightening, and we should be careful not to overdo it.

Still, borrowing in our 20s and 30s is often a rational strategy, allowing us to jumpstart our financial life. After all, if we couldn't borrow and instead had to pay cash for college or for our first home, many of us would have to spend a decade or two scrimping and saving before we notched those two milestones.

Indeed, borrowing to pay for college or technical training can be a smart investment because it can greatly boost our human capital's value. One obvious payback: The resulting larger income will allow us to save more each month. The goal: Amass enough money so one day we can live solely on our financial capital—and we no longer need the income generated by our human capital.

Human factor

How should we invest our savings? We might view our human capital as similar to a bond with its predictable stream of income. That regular income frees us up to invest heavily in the stock market. How much of our portfolio should we stash in stocks? We might ask ourselves three questions.

First, how stable is our job? The more secure it is, the more we could potentially invest in the stock market, knowing it's unlikely we'll need to tap our portfolio to pay for a long period of unemployment. Second, how much will we likely save in total between now and when we retire? We might view those future savings as part of our portfolio's bond and cash holdings, allowing us to be even more aggressive in allocating our portfolio to stocks.

Third, how near are we to retirement? When we get within ten years or so, we'll likely want to boost our portfolio's bond and cash holdings, so we have a pool of conservative investments that we can draw on for spending money and which can replace the soon-to-disappear income generated by our human capital.

What if, during our working years, misfortune strikes and we find ourselves without a paycheck? That might happen if we lose our job, become disabled or fall ill. We might even suffer an untimely demise, leaving our family without any way to support itself. This is the reason to have both an emergency fund and three crucial insurance policies: health, disability and life insurance. We can think of these precautions as protection for our human capital.

Making progress

Our human capital doesn't just allow us to pull in a paycheck. It also offers us the chance to enjoy that pleasant feeling that we're being productive and making progress. Of course, we don't need a job to feel productive. Instead, we might volunteer, or help with the grandchildren, or work on our health, or do countless other things.

Even though my cancer diagnosis means I have limited time left, I still hunger for a sense of progress. I find it hard to devote a day to deliberately doing very little or focusing solely on activities for my own enjoyment. I feel better if I've spent the day being productive, and doubly so if I feel I've been helping others.

I suspect that most folks aren't as restless as I am. But I also suspect almost all of us feel better when we end the day with a sense of accomplishment and devote at least part of the day to activities that help the wider community.

That brings me to retirement. Even after we quit the workforce, we'll likely find we still hunger for the sense that we're being productive, hence my frequent suggestion that folks continue to make use of their human capital during their initial retirement years by working part time.

That part-time position may make for a financially less stressful retirement, while also offering the sense of accomplishment we humans crave. Looking ahead to retirement? To our to-do list, here's one more item to add: Think about how we might continue to make a little money by working a few days each week. Maybe you will ultimately decide that isn't something you want to do during your retirement years. Still, it can't hurt to give it some thought.

Mind Over Money

I like to think I'm rational in the way I spend my dollars, and I suspect most readers do, too. We are, of course, deluding ourselves.

Spending is never simply about buying what we want or need. Instead, behind every dollar that leaves—or doesn't leave—our wallet is a complex mental dance that reflects how we feel that day, the influence of others, how we want to be perceived, and our own financial history. We might declare that we're using our money to buy happiness. But the truth is far more complicated.

To make matters worse, it can be hard to tease out why we're behaving the way we are. How exactly are others influencing us? What precisely are we trying to signal to family and friends with the way we use our dollars? Why were we disciplined yesterday but spending impulsively today? Which of our past financial experiences is driving our behavior?

Want to be a little more sensible in how you deploy your dollars? Here are just some of the things that are likely driving your behavior:

Needs

Folks will declare that they need certain items. But our true needs—basic nutrition, shelter, medical help when sick, transport to our place of work—are pretty modest and, if we were inclined to skimp, would likely devour only a small percentage of our income.

Wants

Because our "needs" are rarely just that, it's often hard to separate them from our "wants." A Caribbean vacation is undoubtedly a want. But what about the imported parmesan that we sprinkle on our salad? It would be hard to argue that it's merely a cheese that delivers part of our daily protein needs.

Mood

Why do folks spend more freely when they're on vacation, or splurge when they've had a rough day at the office, or treat themselves when they feel they've behaved well? Clearly, our mood affects our willingness to spend.

I'm especially intrigued by the idea of a "willpower budget," perhaps because I see it in my own behavior. If it's been a taxing day and my willpower is at a low ebb, I'm much more inclined to eat less healthily at dinner and perhaps have that second glass of wine.

Others

Whether it's the items we buy, the places we vacation or the investments we purchase, we're often influenced by others, whether we know it or not. We might be responding to a casual comment from neighbors or spurred on by the latest corporate advertising blitz. The danger: We're nudged into spending money in ways we later regret or that don't reflect our desires and priorities.

Signaling

Even as we get nudged on our spending, we're also hoping to influence others. Whether it's the second-hand car that says we're frugal or the carefully cultivated garden that says we prize beauty and order, we're constantly trying to tell the world who we are and what we value. And, no, we don't necessarily have to spend to get our message across.

For instance, simply alluding to our portfolio's size or our home's value can boost our standing in the eyes of others.

History

Even as we look to the future, we're all shaped by the past. My parents and grandparents were all careful spenders, whether out of necessity or because they viewed extravagance with distaste.

This was reflected in the family stories that got told. My paternal grandfather would talk about how he was all but starved by the aunt who raised him. My mother often recounts how the great family fortune was frittered away. My father would regale others with his mischievous penny-pinching, such as how he'd use the pool and walking trails at Virginia's Homestead Resort while staying at a nearby motel.

Security

One of money's most important roles is to deliver a comforting sense of financial resilience. That, of course, stems from the dollars we opt not to spend. How much do we need to set aside to feel safe? The answer will vary for each of us.

If we're constantly in danger of getting laid off, it would be rational to keep a fat emergency fund. What if there's scant risk we'll lose our job, but we have visceral childhood memories of our parents struggling to find work? A fat emergency fund might not be a financial necessity for us—but it could still be crucial to our peace of mind.

Future self

We use our dollars not just to buy a sense of short-term financial security, but also to give us confidence about the decades ahead. How concerned are we about our future self, and hence how much are we willing to sacrifice today so we can have a more financially comfortable future? This is a puzzling one, with a minority of folks making ample provision for their later years, while most folks put aside surprisingly little, even as they frequently lament their lack of retirement savings.

Legacy

We save money not just for ourselves, but also for future generations. This isn't just something the wealthy do. How many retirees view their home's value as untouchable, because they want at least that money to go to their kids? It's a sentiment I've heard countless times over the years.

Giving

We give not just to family, but also to others, including charitable organizations and our place of worship. I'd never want to impugn the motive of those who give generously. Still, it's clear that giving can bring as big a smile to the giver as the recipient. Why does generosity make us happy? As with all uses of money, there's no single answer—and instead, for each of us, the challenge is to understand what drives our own behavior.

Taking It Personally

Which financial dangers should we focus on? The possibilities seem pretty much endless, and yet our notion of risk used to be far more circumscribed.

In the late 1980s, when I started writing about personal finance, insurance was considered important, but it wasn't much discussed. Instead, the only risk that seemed to merit serious analysis was investment risk, and that could supposedly be captured by a single, objective measure: volatility.

This approach had intellectual appeal. By focusing on volatility, experts could sidestep a thorny issue—the fact that some investors were totally freaked out by investment price swings, while others remained unperturbed.

As data on historical market returns became more readily available, talk of short-term volatility was joined by discussion of longer-term risk. How likely was an investment to make money over one, five, ten and 20 years? Once again, it was all about the numbers, with investors themselves strangely absent from the conversation.

The good news: Today's discussions of risk are more nuanced, reflecting an awareness that the danger from misfortune is matched by the damage that can be done by our own behavior. Consider the typical stock market cycle. Thanks to research by behavioral finance experts, we now have a pretty good idea of how investors' thinking changes along with the market.

What goes up

The goal of investing may be to buy low and sell high. But at market bottoms, when stocks might be available at 30% or 40% below their bull market peak, we're often frozen in place, fearful our own actions will make matters worse. Sins of commission and sins of omission can both cause financial pain, but sins of commission are much more likely to trigger pangs of regret.

As share prices tick higher, some of us will look to sell, as we recoup part or all of our losses. We're anchored to the price we paid for our investments or to our portfolio's highest value, and we're anxious to sell before recent gains turn to losses once again. It's the old "get even, then get out" syndrome.

Others, meanwhile, take the market's short-term gain and extrapolate it into the future, prompting them to invest even more in stocks. Like the soothsayers of old, we study the market's entrails, trying to divine the future by spotting patterns in today's share-price movements. Our portfolio's rising value makes us more confident not only about the rally, but also about our own investment acumen, as we attribute our gains to our own brilliance.

Among some investors, the rising market may even trigger the so-called house-money effect. What's that? Like casino gamblers who get lucky early in the evening, bull markets can make us feel like we're ahead of the game, prompting us to trade more and take additional risk.

What do we buy? Often, we're drawn to the familiar, such as our employer's shares or companies whose products we use. Alternatively, we might flock to soaring stocks and funds that are in the news or that others are currently raving about.

Taken together, such investments may leave us with a badly diversified portfolio, and yet familiarity and popularity can make these stocks feel like a safe bet. Buoyed by the enthusiasm of others, we end up with a far more aggressive portfolio than we owned at the bull market's inception—setting us up for hefty losses when stocks turn lower.

All fall down

As share prices slide, we shrug off the setback, ignoring negative news and the market's rich valuations. Instead, we seek validation in the words of Wall Street's bullish pundits, taking courage from their upbeat market assessment.

But then stocks' losses deepen, the pundits grow more equivocal and our confidence ebbs away. Initially, we'd expected the decline to reverse. Now, we start extrapolating the losses, wondering how much worse things will get.

At the market's peak, we would boast to others about our high tolerance for risk and our hefty allocation to stocks. But that bravado evaporates along with our portfolio's gains, and now we wish we owned a far less aggressive portfolio.

Enter loss aversion—our tendency to get far more pain from losses than pleasure from gains. Stung by our portfolio's decline, some of us sell in a panic, because our investments are now underwater and we imagine things will get far worse. Alternatively, we might "double down" on our stocks, with an eye to speeding our portfolio's recovery should the market rally—a good move with broad-market index funds, a risky proposition with individual stocks.

But most of us simply sit tight. During the bull market, we took great pride in selling our winners, even if the result was hefty capital-gains taxes. But now that tax losses are readily available, we're loath to take advantage, because we hate the idea of selling for less than we paid. Instead, we comfort ourselves by saying, "They're only paper losses."

What about shoveling more dollars into the stock market? Everything tells us not to: The news is relentlessly bad, the pundits declare that the bear-market bottom could be months away, and the market's decline makes further losses seem inevitable. Stocks may be on sale, our wise neighbor declares that this is a great opportunity and we might even agree—but buying seems simply too risky.

Never Enough

Many financial ideas are tough to embrace. But perhaps the toughest can be summed up in one simple word: enough.

Will we ever feel like we have enough and that we've accomplished enough? Accepting that we have enough and done enough might seem like worthy goals, a serene acceptance that's possible for those at peace with themselves and the world around them. Indeed, for many, "retirement" and "enough" seem to be pretty much synonymous, a declaration that the pursuit of "more" is over.

But that isn't where my head is. Even now, I'm not sure I'll ever declare "I'm done," which is weird, because I sure don't have the time to do much about it.

And I don't think I'm alone. In their 60s, and with decades potentially ahead, I suspect many retirees—and perhaps most—aren't quite done, and I'm not sure it's necessary. There's great pleasure to be had in life's striving. While we might want to temper our pursuit of more, I'm not sure we should seek to squash it entirely.

Amassing more

We spend our lives running on the hedonic treadmill, imagining the next accomplishment—the new house, the seven-figure portfolio, the promotion—is all that stands between us and happiness, only to discover that success soon leaves us dissatisfied and hankering after something else.

This desire for more doesn't seem to disappear with retirement.

Most of us spend three-plus decades amassing money to fund our post-work life and yet, when the time comes, we're often reluctant to let our dollars go.

Such reluctance is understandable. After a lifetime of saving, it's hard to watch our money slip away. And if an ever-growing portfolio brings someone happiness, why should the rest of us object? Still, the desire for more can create two key problems.

First, in their pursuit of an ever-larger portfolio, retirees might take too much risk—and imperil their financial future. Second, folks may shortchange their retirement by failing to spend in ways that could enhance their happiness during their final years. This, I think, is one virtue of Social Security benefits, pensions, immediate fixed annuities and laddered bond portfolios. All are designed to generate income, so folks feel they have permission to spend the money involved.

Struggling to let go of the dollars you've amassed? Consider making gifts to charity and loved ones. These aren't just an alternative to spending. Such gifts are also an acknowledgment that we have enough—and the resulting sense of abundance may prompt us to be more generous with ourselves.

Scoring goals

Even as we struggle to accept that we've amassed enough, we're also reluctant to declare that we've done enough.

Humans are a restless, relentless bunch, always looking to improve their lives in one way or another. This drive, I'd argue, is a good thing: It not only helps the individuals involved, but also it can spur economic growth and make society a better place for everyone.

Yes, retirees and those near the end of their career will often proclaim that they've reached the point where they've done enough, and they're now happy to cruise through their remaining years. But I'm not sure I believe them.

These folks might be content to step off the workplace hamster wheel. But retirees often replace their professional aspirations with goals of their own choosing, such as reading a book every week, or visiting all 50 U.S. states, or pursuing their favorite hobby. And I see nothing wrong with that. There's great happiness to be had from accomplishment.

Will we ever feel like we've done enough? I suspect not. We might be willing to declare that we're done with career goals, but I doubt most of us will ever feel like we have nothing left to achieve.

Still, we might try to cut ourselves a little slack, especially as we age. How? I like to make a daily to-do list, preferably one that isn't too long, so I know what success looks like for that day. Clearing each day's list allows me to head into the evening with a pleasurable sense of accomplishment—and the chance to recharge and reflect before tackling the next day's list.

What's It All About?

We're always striving—the next pay raise, the next consumer purchase, the next self-improvement goal. But to what end?

Our time on this earth is fleeting, our impact minimal and our legacy quickly forgotten. A decade after we're gone, we might be remembered by family and close friends, but not by many others. And yet we keep pushing forward.

Does death's approach shed any light on this curious behavior? Far from it. If anything, my cancer diagnosis has pushed me to strive even more. You might dismiss this as denial of what's certain to come or perhaps a desperate grab for control in a world where I no longer have much say over my destiny.

Alternatively, you might view this as some mix of selfishness and selflessness. For the religiously inclined, perhaps I'm aiming to leave the world very marginally better for the sake of God's glory and my own immortal soul. For the more secular, maybe my goal is to ensure my family—and hence my genes—have a better shot at surviving and reproducing.

But while I'm not sure what propels my continued striving, even at this late stage, I know it makes me feel better. Accomplishment can deliver great happiness. That brings me to the final article I wrote for *The Wall Street Journal* before I left in 2008 to work for six years at Citigroup, or what my journalism friends would call "the dark side."

In that piece, I listed what I felt were the three components of a happy life: a sense of security, the freedom to pursue our passions, and a robust network of friends and family.

We all want slightly different versions of these things, but I believe the hunger for all three is almost universal. Together, they have the potential to leave us feeling safe, fulfilled and happy—innate desires that we carry with us throughout our life.

Do pursuing these three things make the world a better place? Perhaps marginally. They certainly don't seem like pursuits that should hurt those around us.

Meanwhile, they help to make each day that much sweeter. And ever since I got my cancer diagnosis, that has been my goal: I want every day to be a good day.

Faced with my grim diagnosis, I've refused to be angry about my misfortune, or dwell on why I got unlucky, or rail about the years I won't have. Why waste time on such emotions? Instead, my focus has been on making the most of the days I have left.

No, not every day has been happy. Life's hassles have a way of intruding, and those hassles have grated even more because my time is short. Meanwhile, deteriorating health is obviously no fun.

On top of that, those around me have bad days, and their distress inevitably taints my waking hours. But I view this unhappiness differently. Unlike the hassle of leaking toilets or the distress of failing health, sadness—whether it's our own or that of others—is part of the human experience, and adds a richness to it. With shared sadness, we can draw closer to others, and those tighter human connections can make life more meaningful.

Over the decades, I've written a lot about money and happiness, and yet "happiness" has always struck me as the wrong word, and academic alternatives like "subjective well-being" and "life satisfaction" don't seem any better.

Yes, happiness is a key component of a good life, but it's hardly the only one. Instead, robust happiness encompasses not just laughter and good times, but also feeling fulfilled, a sense of purpose, a passion for life, a sense of contentment, and a feeling we're engaged both with others and with the broader world. It's the sense we're truly alive and focused on what we really want and care about. Such things, I believe, are always worth striving for—even when our time is measured not in decades, but in weeks and months.

10.
Farewell
Friends

A scan in early October 2024 revealed a pulmonary embolism. That's when I learned cancer can lead to blood clots—and those clots may mean an earlier demise. It was yet another wake-up call, telling me I needed to prepare for my own death. When I returned home after 48 hours in the hospital and with a prescription for blood thinners, I wrote the piece below, with instructions to Elaine to publish it on HumbleDollar after my death.

IF THIS POST is appearing, it means I've succumbed to cancer or one of its side effects. Please don't feel sad for me. I've had a life filled with love, great experiences and wonderful career opportunities. Despite my demise at a relatively young age, I consider myself beyond fortunate.

I'm hoping that, under the tree in front of our little Philadelphia rowhome, my wife Elaine will place a stone tablet inscribed with my name, and the year I was born and died. Underneath, I'd like the tablet to read:

Family • Readers • Words

(Note to Elaine: If you ever move, feel free to take the tablet with you.)

Family is everybody who's brought love into my life: Elaine, my two children, my larger family, my close friends. Meanwhile, readers have been those I've served, and who rewarded that service with so much loyalty and affection. Finally, words have been my playground, taking the insights I've garnered and trying to make them understandable to others. Beside the tree are two old metal chairs. I hope family and passersby will occasionally stop by, and fill me in on what I've been missing.

I've asked Elaine to arrange a memorial service at St. Peter's Church in Philadelphia's Old City. She'll post the time and date to HumbleDollar when the details have been worked out.

Regular readers will know much of my life's story. But I figure it's appropriate to offer a not-so-brief recap.

I was born at 14 St Margaret's Drive in Twickenham, London, on January 2, 1963. At that time in the UK, it was standard practice for mothers to give birth in the hospital if it was their first child—or, in my mother's case, her first two children. My older brothers, who are identical twins, had been born two years earlier. Because that first delivery went smoothly, my birth would be at home. From what I gather, the midwife took cigarette and Scotch breaks with my father during lulls in the action. I was born at 6 a.m., thus establishing a lifetime habit of starting early.

In 1966, my father left financial journalism for a job at the World Bank, and we moved from London to Washington, DC. Two years later, my younger sister was born. In late 1972, my father was posted to the World Bank's Bangladesh office for four years, and I was dispatched to boarding school in England, joining my two brothers.

After the comforts of a U.S. suburban childhood, it was a brutal change—cold dormitories, disgusting food, endless bullying—and I carried the scars for the rest of my life. But there was a silver lining: After nine years of boarding school, I squeaked into Cambridge University, where I spent much of my three years writing for and editing the student newspaper.

When I graduated Cambridge in 1985, the UK economy was in rough shape and landing a job was difficult. I ended up working for *Euromoney* magazine in London. Initially, all went well. But then there was a change in editor and, for reasons I never understood, the new editor took an instant dislike to me and made it clear he wanted me gone. But by then, I'd already decided to leave London and return to the U.S.

My then-fiancee and I flew to New York in August 1986. After a desperate scramble, I landed a job as a reporter—read "fact checker"—at *Forbes* magazine. The pay was miserable, but I couldn't have been more grateful for that first paycheck. By then, all I had to my name was credit card debt.

Molly and I were married the following June, and Hannah arrived 15 months later. Her younger brother, Henry, would follow in 1992.

After 23 months as a fact checker, I was promoted to staff writer at *Forbes*, covering mutual funds. *The Wall Street Journal,* which was also in need of a funds reporter, came calling 16 months later. I'd always thought I'd never be a real journalist until I worked for a daily newspaper, and yet initially I said "no."

At the time, I was in the midst of six months as a single parent, looking after Hannah on my own while Molly was in Syria, Greece and Turkey conducting research for her PhD. Still, the *Journal* wasn't deterred, saying it would make allowances during my initial months.

In the early 1990s, the *Journal* was very different from the newspaper it is today. No photos, just the dot drawings for which the paper was renowned. While strong opinions could be found on the editorial page, they were to be avoided in the news pages. The sort of advice journalism I favored was frowned upon by some among the paper's senior ranks.

Still, in 1994, Managing Editor Paul Steiger said he'd consider a few columnists for the *Journal's* news pages. At age 31, and with some trepidation, I put up my hand. Thus was born the "Getting Going" column, which I wrote for the next 13-plus years, penning 1,009 columns for both *The Wall Street Journal* and *Wall Street Journal Sunday.* The latter consisted of branded pages that appeared in some 70 newspapers around the country.

In retrospect, it's astonishing that I was given my own column at such a young age. It took me a few months to hit my stride, but

I was soon pounding away at the virtues of index funds, while also exploring new topics, often scouring academic research for insights I could share with readers.

The decade and a half that followed are something of a blur. I was cranking out columns, commuting into New York City from the New Jersey suburbs, and raising two children. In my memory, the years have the monotony of a hamster wheel. But that wasn't the reality: There were high points and low points, plus the joy of watching Hannah and Henry grow up. The low points included the World Trade Center attack, my father's death and a libel suit brought against the *Journal*. I'd been involved in editing the story that triggered the lawsuit.

In early 1995, while in Pittsburgh, I went on a nine-mile run with my brother-in-law, who was training for the city's marathon. I'd long viewed running those 26.2 miles as a heroic endeavor. I committed to returning for the next year's marathon. But I didn't simply want to complete the distance. Instead, I set a goal of finishing in under three hours. I managed it, though barely, crossing the finish line 24 seconds under the three-hour mark.

I ran countless road races over the next dozen years. I had my greatest success with half-marathons, finishing third in the four races I ran on land—and first in the 2001 half-marathon held on the deck of a boat floating off Antarctica. In shorter races, from one mile to ten, I also managed perhaps a dozen first-place finishes. What about the tearful, wimpy English schoolboy who had previously shunned athletic endeavors? Over countless miles, I managed to leave him behind.

Career and athletic success were not, alas, rivaled by relationship success. Molly announced she wanted a divorce in 1998. It would be the first of two failed marriages—not an achievement I'm proud of. But the third time was a charm. In the midst of the pandemic, Elaine and I met in August 2020, the month my second marriage officially ended. We were living together by the end of the month and married almost four years later, in May 2024, five days after my cancer diagnosis. I met Elaine during one of my life's roughest periods, and was so lucky to have done so. Elaine, I fear, was not so fortunate, for now she must navigate the world on her own.

By 2006 or so, I'd started to tire of the "Getting Going" column, and began casting around for what to do next. I had a few conversations with potential employers, but those came to naught. Then, one day in early 2008, my phone rang. It was Andy Seig from Citigroup. He was heading up a start-up within Citi known as myFi, which was aiming to deliver advice on a client's entire financial life in return for a flat monthly fee. It was, I imagined, the exit from the *Journal* I was looking for.

I joined myFi that spring, and it soon became apparent that launching a start-up in the middle of a huge corporate bureaucracy was a foolhardy endeavor. Layered on top of that was the financial crisis that unfolded through the year. By mid-2009, myFi was dead, and we employees spent a long, aimless summer trying to figure out what was next.

Next turned out to be a new wealth management operation cobbled together by combining myFi's remaining employees, who had been hired to launch an innovative new financial service, and the old school brokers who sat in Citi's bank branches. It wasn't exactly a match made in heaven.

I toughed it out at Citi until spring 2014. Money was undoubtedly part of the reason. I was making more than $300,000 a year, a gaudy sum for a onetime ink-stained wretch. And the job wasn't without interest. As director of financial education for the U.S. wealth management business, I gave more than 30 speeches in some years— forcing me to overcome my fear of public speaking—and I was dealing with financial topics I'd rarely written about as a journalist, while also learning about the investment business from the inside. Still, I was also frustrated by the nit-picky oversight of lawyers and compliance officers, and vowed to leave.

For a year, I planned my departure, getting my finances in order and setting in motion some work projects for my life after Citi. I waited until I got my final year-end bonus in early 2014, and then handed in my notice.

What followed was a period I came to call my second childhood. Initially, that meant a 15-month return to *The Wall Street Journal* as a freelance columnist—I left when my editor got ousted during a round of layoffs in 2015—and also working on two annual editions of the *Jonathan Clements Money Guide*. That guide eventually became the core of HumbleDollar, which I launched on December 31, 2016.

The two printed editions of the money guide were among the nine books I wrote over my career—eight personal finance books and a novel. I also edited two books, including *My Money Journey*, a compilation of 30 essays by HumbleDollar writers, and contributed essays to a fistful of other tomes, including penning the foreword to two Bill Bernstein books. None of the books I authored was a huge success. But my favorite, and the one with the best sales, was my 2016 book, *How to Think About Money*.

In 2016, I was also contacted by Peter Mallouk, president of fast-growing Creative Planning, a registered investment advisor that favored index funds and sought to help clients with their entire financial life. As at Citi, I was again given the title of director of financial education, though I remained an independent contractor and worked limited hours for Creative. Still, for me, it proved to be one of my career's most enjoyable professional relationships. Peter was great to work with, and together we hosted a monthly podcast that ran for the rest of my life.

By May 2024, I'd been living in Philadelphia for more than three years, I was engaged to Elaine and living just an eight-minute walk from my daughter, son-in-law and two grandsons. The youngest was born that month. Elaine and I were talking about retirement, trying to figure out how we could travel more and have more time for each other, even as I kept HumbleDollar humming along.

And then I got my cancer diagnosis.

The period immediately after was astonishingly busy, as I tried to get my affairs in order and prep HumbleDollar for a life without me, even as my diagnosis triggered a surprising amount of media attention. *The New York Times* wrote about my illness, I was interviewed for Consuelo Mack's *WealthTrack*, and I was asked to pen articles for *The Washington Post*, *The Telegraph* of London, *The Wall Street Journal* and *AARP The Magazine*. Who knew that candor about one's own death would generate so much interest? It was an odd bookend to a life spent partly in the public eye—one that had previously been most notable for pounding the table for index funds.

I faced the final months not with sorrow, but with great gratitude. I had spent almost my entire adult life doing what I love and surrounded by those that I love.

Who could ask for more?

About the Author

Jonathan Clements was the founder and editor of personal finance website HumbleDollar.com. Born in England and educated at Cambridge University, he spent almost 20 years at *The Wall Street Journal* in New York, where he was the newspaper's personal finance columnist, and six years at Citigroup, where he was director of financial education for the bank's U.S. wealth management arm. Jonathan wrote, edited and contributed to numerous personal finance books, including the award-winning *How to Think About Money* and *My Money Journey*.